# Pattern Recognition - Selected Methods and Applications

*Edited by Andrzej Zak*

Published in London, United Kingdom

IntechOpen

*Supporting open minds since 2005*

Pattern Recognition - Selected Methods and Applications
http://dx.doi.org/10.5772/intechopen.75291
Edited by Andrzej Zak

Contributors
Mahmoud Ghofrani, Rasool Azimi, Ihab Zaqout, David Horn, Pavel Viktorovich Smirnov, Alexander Tashlinskii, Wen-Liang Hwang, Shih-Shuo Tung, Ngan Le, Marios Savvides, Khoa Lu, Andrzej Zak



First published in London, United Kingdom, 2019 by IntechOpen
IntechOpen is the global imprint of INTECHOPEN LIMITED, registered in England and Wales, registration number: 11086078, The Shard, 25th floor, 32 London Bridge Street
London, SE19SG – United Kingdom
Printed in Croatia

British Library Cataloguing-in-Publication Data
A catalogue record for this book is available from the British Library

Additional hard and PDF copies can be obtained from orders@intechopen.com

Pattern Recognition - Selected Methods and Applications
Edited by Andrzej Zak
p. cm.
Print ISBN 978-1-78985-499-2
Online ISBN 978-1-78985-500-5
eBook (PDF) ISBN 978-1-83880-395-7

# Meet the editor

Dr. Andrzej Zak comes from Poland. He graduated from the Military University of Technology with a Master of Science engineering degree in Computer Science. In the Polish Naval Academy, Dr. Zak did his degree of Doctor of Technical Sciences and the AGH University of Science and Technology awarded him a degree of doctor habilitated in technical science in the field of automation and robotics in the specialization of autonomous underwater vehicles. His research area deals with issues related to the control of dynamic systems and the broadly understood hydroacoustics, especially data transmission and object detection and identification based on passive measurements. Dr. Zak has published many articles and conference papers covering topics related directly or indirectly to pattern recognition.

# Contents

# Preface

The impact of pattern recognition on the improvement of human life cannot go unnoticed. Additionally, its unique qualities have aroused considerable interest and are desired by the military, many governmental institutions and state offices, as well as ordinary people.

Significantly, systems of pattern recognition are becoming increasingly applicable in many areas with various studies on new methods and prototypes being carried out in different countries now reaching thousands. Pattern recognition combined with biometrics creates security systems that protect objects from unauthorized persons on the one hand andsystems that support the protection of significant state infrastructure facilities such as airports, ports, and many more on the other. In medicine, pattern recognition helps diagnosticians and doctors to detect abnormal lesions and disease outbreaks, and create systems for early diagnosis of diseases. Technical sciences among others use pattern recognition in the identification of prefailure states. One could point to hundreds of other applications. The wide application of pattern recognition in many areas of human activity is now more than obvious. Unlocking our smartphone with a fingerprint or showing our face would not be possible without pattern recognition methods. This has resulted in the design of novel methods, algorithms, and systems that are directly or indirectly connected with pattern recognition.

I hope that this book will contribute to the propagation and further development of knowledge in the field of pattern recognition.

**Andrzej Zak**
Polish Naval Academy, Gdynia, Poland

Chapter 1

# Introductory Chapter: Pattern Recognition as Cognitive Process

*Andrzej Zak*

## 1. Introduction

The development of science and rapid advances in technology have created many new problems that mankind is currently encountering. The solution to the majority of these problems is based on information processing. We can easily say that without information processing, our civilization, in the form we know, could not exist, and information is a key element of the decision-making process. Decision-making is inextricably linked to the automation of various processes. Currently, the trend is automated by performing operations with the characteristics of intelligence, which until now were performed only by people. An example here can be systems that have speech recognition capabilities, images recognition (reading hand-writing letters and signature recognition), people recognition (biometric systems), text translations, chess games, proofs of claims, and many others. The basis for solving these tasks is methods for pattern recognition.

The concept of pattern recognition is difficult to define unequivocally. The laconic definition will be too short to reflect the nature and essence of the concept. In turn, a too long definition causes the blurring of the essence of the problem. Pattern recognition is a scientific issue that has its roots among others in information theory, mathematical analysis and statistics, signal and image processing, machine learning, artificial intelligence, and many others. The possibilities of implementing algorithms from this area as well as the application potential of the developed solutions mean that this field of knowledge is most often identified with automation and robotics, mechatronics, and computer science. The methods, algorithms, and tools used in other scientific areas, e.g., artificial neural networks, optimization methods, genetic and evolutionary algorithms, fuzzy logic, etc., are often used to create and implement practical solutions in the field of pattern recognition. The pattern recognition process itself can be treated as an action consisting in retrieving raw data and taking further actions depending on the category to which these data belong.

It is most commonly assumed that the main areas of application of pattern recognition in the field of technical sciences are signal and image analysis systems. However, it should be noted that pattern recognition can be successfully used in medical sciences, e.g., in the identification of diseases or in social sciences, e.g., when recognizing the behavior of each individual or a group.

Recognition of patterns aims at classifying objects based on statistical data collected for the purpose of extracting features of objects based on a priori information or using self-learning. Classified objects are usually groups of measurement or observation results defining the location of corresponding points in the multidimensional space of features. In other words, pattern recognition is a procedure in which individual items are placed into groups based on quantitative information on one or more characteristics inherent in the items (referred to as traits, variables, characters, etc.) and based on a training set of previously labeled items.

In general, the pattern recognition system consists of several elements. The first element is a sensor that provides information from observations of a certain physical phenomenon that will be subject to classification or description. Information from the sensor is most often transformed into a digital form, which can be processed using a microprocessor system. The next elements are usually programmatic or data structures and may or may not be as needed. In their composition, one can distinguish the block responsible for filtration, quality improvement, or pre-processing of information to the desired form. The next block is associated with the mechanism of extracting features that best characterize and separate the class to which the observational data belongs. An indispensable element of the entire system is the decision-making scheme that implements the correct part of the classification or description of the observation process based on the acquired features of the object. This process can be carried out in two ways. In the approach in which the so-called supervised learning is used during the creation of the system, a priori knowledge is required, on the basis of which decisions about classification are made. In the approach in which the so-called supervised learning is used during the creation of the system, a priori knowledge is required, on the basis of which decisions about classification are made. This knowledge is usually collected and stored in a kind of database, which can be supplied with information from outside or by the system itself. In the approach where it is assumed that the system will self-organize and/or self-learn, it is not required to have initial knowledge about the observed object. The number and variety of elements included in the recognition system give a picture of how many issues should be considered to obtain efficiently operating pattern recognition systems.

The beginnings of recognizing patterns and in particular the possibilities of automating the classification process fall on the 1950s and are associated with the slow spreading of digital machines as information processing means. At that time, work in this area focused on the development of methods and algorithms, implementation of signal processing programs including images and automatic decision-making, and the creation of research equipment necessary to obtain information about the object. At that time, among others, a Dreyfus-Graf phonetograph was developed, i.e., a phone recording machine and AUDREY—a Bell machine that recognized numbers. At the end of the 1950s, F. Rosenblatt presented a system called a perceptron that had a significant impact on the development of learning systems. The algorithm describing the operation of the perceptron was one of the first models of brain activity in the field of information storage and processing. During this period, pattern recognition mainly used theories of static decisions and threshold logic. In subsequent years, research in the field of pattern recognition has accelerated with the launch of the digital machines, thereby increasing their performance computing. From the 1960s, we can call a Shoebox machine demonstrated by IBM which recognized 16 words of English, including 10 digits or a reader of reports sent to the Social Security Administration in the US that can read printed letters regardless of the thickness of characters or print quality. In subsequent years, methods, algorithms, and software for recognizing images and sounds were developed. In addition to technical sciences, other types of sciences have become interested in pattern recognition, such as medicine, sociology, psychology, archeology, and many others. Currently, these methods are very common; we use them almost every day, often without such awareness, even during unlocking smartphones with a fingerprint or showing face.

The main objective of this book is to present the latest achievements in the field of pattern recognition and a better understanding of the involved key issues. Moreover, the presented practical solutions of problems allow the same to become familiar with the technical and non-technical aspects of various applications as well as the latest developments in this area. For this reason, scientists from research institutions and universities of various countries of the world present their achievements in the field of pattern recognition. According to the information presented in this book, the impact of pattern recognition systems on the improvement of human life is invaluable in particular due to the wide field of application. It must be noticed that many of the ideas, methods, and algorithms presented in this book can be applied in other applications. I hope that this book will bring some of the problems associated with pattern recognition and will be an inspiration for further research. I also hope that this publication will be received by the scientific community with great interest.

## Author details

Andrzej Zak
Polish Naval Academy, Gdynia, Poland

*Address all correspondence to: a.zak@amw.gdynia.pl

Chapter 2

# Formation of Inter-Frame Deformation Field of Images Using Reverse Stochastic Gradient Estimation

*Alexander Tashlinskii and Pavel Smirnov*


## Abstract

The effectiveness of the use of stochastic gradient estimation to detect motion in a sequence of images is investigated. Pixel-by-pixel reverse estimation of the deformation field is used. The representation of the shift vector is considered both by the projections on the basic axes and by the polar parameters. Two approaches to estimate the parameters of the deformation field are proposed and analyzed. In the first approach, the stochastic gradient procedure sequentially processes all rows of an image to find estimates of shifts for all points of the reference image. The joint processing of the results allows compensating the inertia of the stochastic estimation. In the second approach, to improve the accuracy of estimation, the correlation of image rows is taken into account. As a criterion for the formation of the resulting estimate, the minimum of gradient estimation and correlation maximum were investigated. The computational complexity of the proposed algorithms is investigated. The algorithms are compared with the MVFAST algorithm. Examples of experimental results on the formation of the deformation field, the selection of a moving object area, and the finding of the movement and trajectory parameters of a moving object in a video sequence are given.


**Keywords:** image processing, video sequence, motion, shift vector, detection, stochastic estimation, stochastic gradient, trajectory, reverse estimation, correlation

## 1. Introduction

One of the challenges in video processing is moving object detection and tracking. Some tasks require only detection of the motion, while others require extraction of the moving object or the motion area boundary. The biggest challenge is to estimate trajectory parameters of a moving object in a video sequence. A solution quality to the problem largely depends on the accuracy of moving object area detection, since all the information needed to determine motion parameters and trajectory of the object is extracted from the image.

There are various approaches to identify the area of moving object based on the inter-frame difference [1, 2], background subtraction [2, 3], the use of statistics [2, 4], block estimation [5], and optical flow analysis [6]. The processing can be presented as estimation of inter-frame geometric deformations of two images, one of which can be considered as the reference image $\mathbf{Z}^{\mathrm{s}} = \left\{z^{\mathrm{s}}_{i,j}\right\}$ and the second as deformed image $\mathbf{Z}^{\mathrm{d}} = \left\{z^{\mathrm{d}}_{i,j}\right\}$, where $z^{*}_{i,j}$ is the value in node $(i,j)$ of the image. The field $\mathbf{H} = \left\{\overline{h}_{i,j}\right\}$ of inter-frame shift vectors $\overline{h}_{i,j}$ of all points of the reference image corresponding to the nodes of the sample grid will be called deformation field or shift vectors' field.

An important task of estimating the trajectory of a moving object is to increase the spatial accuracy of detecting the area of motion in an image sequence. The solution of this problem depends on the quality of estimation of the deformation field. When finding estimates of shifts for each node of the deformed image, the approach of using stochastic gradient estimation [7–9] is promising. It finds coordinates $(x,y)$ of points of the reference image on the deformed image. That is, it evaluates vectors $\overline{h}_{i,j} = \left(h_{(i,j)x}, h_{(i,j)y}\right)^T$ of inter-frame shifts of points $(i,j)$ (**Figure 1**) of the reference image.

In view of the insignificant change in brightness on adjacent frames of a video sequence, it is advisable to use mean square inter-frame difference as the objective function of estimation. Then, for the projections, $h_{(i,j)x}$ and $h_{(i,j)y}$ of shift vector, we get [10]

$$\hat{\overline{h}}_{i,j+1} = \hat{\overline{h}}_{i,j} - \lambda_h \,\mathrm{sign}\left(\overline{\beta}_h\left(z^{\mathrm{d}}_{i,j+1}, \hat{\overline{h}}_{i,j}\right)\right), i = \overline{1, N_x}, j = \overline{1, N_y - 1}, \qquad (1)$$

where $\lambda_h$ is the learning rate, which determines the rate of change of the estimated parameters, $\overline{\beta}_h = \left(\beta_{hx}, \beta_{hy}\right)^T$ is the gradient estimation of an objective function, and $N_x \times N_y$ is the image size.

The projections of stochastic gradient can be represented as [11]

$$\beta_{hx} = \left(\tilde{z}^{\mathrm{s}}_{x+\Delta x, y} - \tilde{z}^{\mathrm{s}}_{x-\Delta x, y}\right)\left(\tilde{z}^{\mathrm{s}}_{x,y} - z^{\mathrm{d}}_{i,j}\right),$$

$$\beta_{hy} = \left(\tilde{z}^{\mathrm{s}}_{x, y+\Delta y} - \tilde{z}^{\mathrm{s}}_{x, y-\Delta y}\right)\left(\tilde{z}^{\mathrm{s}}_{x,y} - z^{\mathrm{d}}_{i,j}\right),$$

where $(x,y)$ are the coordinates of the reference image point on the deformed image, $\tilde{z}^{\mathrm{s}}_{x,y}$ is the brightness of the continuous image $\tilde{\mathrm{Z}}$s obtained from $\mathbf{Z}^{\mathrm{s}}$ by means of interpolation, and $\Delta x$, $\Delta y$ are the steps of finding estimates of derivatives $\mathrm{d}\tilde{z}^{\mathrm{s}}_{x,y}/\mathrm{d}x$ and $\mathrm{d}\tilde{z}^{\mathrm{s}}_{x,y}/\mathrm{d}y$ [12].

Note that inter-frame shift vector $\overline{h}_{i,j}$ can be also represented in polar form: $\overline{h}_{i,j} = \left(\rho_{i,j}, \varphi_{i,j}\right)$ (**Figure 1**), where $\rho_{i,j}$ is the length of the vector and $\varphi_{i,j}$ is the angle with respect to the $x$ axis (**Figure 1**). Functionally, these representations are equivalent. However, due to the inertia of estimates of shift vectors' field **H**, when using

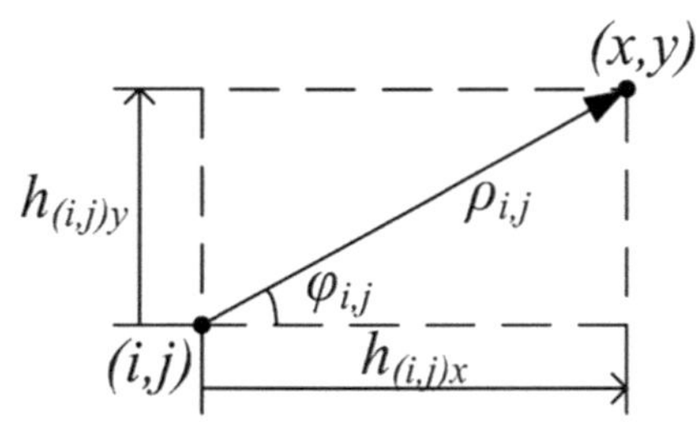


**Figure 1.**
*Representation of shift of reference image point $(i,j)$.*

stochastic gradient descent, the use of parameters $\rho_{i,j}$ and $\varphi_{i,j}$ does not give equivalent estimates $\hat{\overline{h}}_{i,j}$ compared with the use of $h_{(i,j)x}$ and $h_{(i,j)y}$. This is due to the fact that the sets of parameters have different physical meanings [13]. The answer to the question of which set is preferable for solving the problem of moving object area detection is not obvious and requires research.

## 2. Variants of estimation algorithms

Let us compare the efficiency of moving object area identification using the sets of parameters $(h_x, h_y)$ and $(\rho, \varphi)$. The following method for estimating the shift vectors' field **H** is used. At the first stage, stochastic gradient descent algorithm sequentially processes all nodes of the reference image row by row with the set of parameters $(h_x, h_y)$. It processes each row $i$ bidirectionally [14], first, from the left to the right, getting, according to Eq. (1), the estimates

$$\hat{h}^l_{(i,j+1)x} = \hat{h}^l_{(i,j)x} - \lambda_h \operatorname{sign}\left(\beta_{hx}\left(z^{\mathrm{d}}_{i,j+1}, \hat{\overline{h}}_{i,j}\right)\right), \hat{h}^l_{(i,1)x} = \hat{h}^l_{(i-1,1)x},$$

$$\hat{h}^l_{(i,j+1)y} = \hat{h}^l_{(i,j)y} - \lambda_h \operatorname{sign}\left(\beta_{hy}\left(z^{\mathrm{d}}_{i,j+1}, \hat{\overline{h}}_{i,j}\right)\right), \hat{h}^l_{(i,1)y} = \hat{h}^l_{(i-1,1)y},$$

and then from the right to the left getting the estimates

$$\hat{h}^r_{(i,N_y-j)x} = \hat{h}^r_{(i,N_y-j+1)x} - \lambda_h \operatorname{sign}\left(\beta_{hx}\left(z^{\mathrm{d}}_{i,N_y-j}, \hat{\overline{h}}_{i,N_y-j+1}\right)\right), \hat{h}^r_{(i,N_y)x} = \hat{h}^r_{(i-1,N_y)x},$$

$$\hat{h}^r_{(i,N_y-j)y} = \hat{h}^r_{(i,N_y-j+1)y} - \lambda_h \operatorname{sign}\left(\beta_{hy}\left(z^{\mathrm{d}}_{i,N_y-j}, \hat{\overline{h}}_{i,N_y-j+1}\right)\right), \hat{h}^r_{(i,N_y)y} = \hat{h}^r_{(i-1,N_y)y},$$

where parameter $\lambda_h$ is determined by the maximum speed of moving objects.

When using the set of parameters $(\rho, \varphi)$, considering that $\partial x/\partial\rho = \cos\varphi$, $\partial x/\partial\varphi = -\rho\sin\varphi$, $\partial y/\partial\rho = \sin\varphi$, and $\partial y/\partial\varphi = \rho\cos\varphi$, for gradient estimation $\overline{\beta} = (\beta_\rho, \beta_\varphi)^T$, we get [11]

$$\begin{aligned}\beta_\rho = {} & \left(\tilde{z}^{\mathrm{s}}_{x+\Delta x,y} - \tilde{z}^{\mathrm{s}}_{x-\Delta x,y}\right)\left(\tilde{z}^{\mathrm{s}}_{x+\Delta x,y} + \tilde{z}^{\mathrm{s}}_{x-\Delta x,y} - 2z^{\mathrm{d}}_{i,j}\right)\cos\varphi \\ & + \left(\tilde{z}^{\mathrm{s}}_{x,y+\Delta y} - \tilde{z}^{\mathrm{s}}_{x,y-\Delta y}\right)\left(\tilde{z}^{\mathrm{s}}_{x,y+\Delta y} + \tilde{z}^{\mathrm{s}}_{x,y-\Delta y} - 2z^{\mathrm{d}}_{i,j}\right)\sin\varphi, \\ \beta_\varphi = {} & -\left(\tilde{z}^{\mathrm{s}}_{x+\Delta x,y} - \tilde{z}^{\mathrm{s}}_{x-\Delta x,y}\right)\left(\tilde{z}^{\mathrm{s}}_{x+\Delta x,y} + \tilde{z}^{\mathrm{s}}_{x-\Delta x,y} - 2z^{\mathrm{d}}_{i,j}\right)\rho\sin\varphi \\ & + \left(\tilde{z}^{\mathrm{s}}_{x,y+\Delta y} - \tilde{z}^{\mathrm{s}}_{x,y-\Delta y}\right)\left(\tilde{z}^{\mathrm{s}}_{x,y+\Delta y} + \tilde{z}^{\mathrm{s}}_{x,y-\Delta y} - 2z^{\mathrm{d}}_{i,j}\right)\rho\cos\varphi.\end{aligned}$$

Then according to Eq. (1), we get the estimates

$$\hat{\rho}^l_{i,j+1} = \hat{\rho}^l_{i,j} - \lambda_\rho \operatorname{sign}\left(\beta_\rho\left(z^{\mathrm{d}}_{i,j+1}, \hat{\rho}_{i,j}, \hat{\varphi}_{i,j}\right)\right),$$

$$\hat{\varphi}^l_{i,j+1} = \hat{\varphi}^l_{i,j} - \lambda_\varphi \operatorname{sign}\left(\beta_\varphi\left(z^{\mathrm{d}}_{i,j+1}, \hat{\rho}_{i,j}, \hat{\varphi}_{i,j}\right)\right),$$

$$\hat{\rho}^r_{i,N_y-j} = \hat{\rho}^r_{i,N_y-j+1} - \lambda_\rho \operatorname{sign}\left(\beta_\rho\left(z^{\mathrm{d}}_{i,N_y-j}, \hat{\rho}_{i,N_y-j+1}, \hat{\varphi}_{i,N_y-j+1}\right)\right),$$

$$\hat{\varphi}^r_{i,N_y-j} = \hat{\varphi}^r_{i,N_y-j+1} - \lambda_\varphi \operatorname{sign}\left(\beta_\varphi\left(z^{\mathrm{d}}_{i,N_y-j}, \hat{\rho}_{i,N_y-j+1}, \hat{\varphi}_{i,N_y-j+1i,j}\right)\right),$$

where the parameters $\lambda_\rho$ and $\lambda_\varphi$ are also determined by the maximum speed of moving objects.

At the second stage, for each node $(i,j)$, the estimates $\hat{h}^{l}_{(i,j)x}$ and $\hat{h}^{r}_{(i,j)x}$ are processed jointly [15]. The optimal value of $\hat{h}_{(i,j)x}$ is found between the estimates with some step $\Delta_h$. Step $\Delta_h$ is determined by the required accuracy. If the absolute difference between the estimates $\hat{h}^{l}_{(i,j)x}$ and $\hat{h}^{r}_{(i,j)x}$ is less than $\Delta_h$, then the estimate $\hat{h}_{(i,j)x}$ of the deformation parameter is assumed to be equal $\hat{h}^{l}_{(i,j)x}$. Otherwise, the set of possible values of the deformation parameter estimate is given by

$$\hat{h}^{m}_{(i,j)x} = \hat{h}^{l}_{(i,j)x} + m\Delta_h, m = \overline{0, k+1}, k = \left|\hat{h}^{r}_{(i,j)x} - \hat{h}^{l}_{(i,j)x}\right| / \Delta_h.$$

The optimal value of $\hat{h}_{(i,j)x}$ from the resulting set is found using some criterion.

## 2.1 Criteria for the formation of the resulting estimation

Two criteria for the formation of the resulting estimation are studied [16]:

- Gradient estimation minimum

$$\min_{m=\overline{0,\,k+1}} \beta_h\left(\hat{h}^{l}_{(i,j)x} + m\Delta_h\right), \tag{2}$$

- Correlation coefficient maximum (CC)

$$\max_{m=\overline{0,\,k+1}} CC\ \left\{\tilde{z}^{\mathrm{s}}_{x(m)+p,y(m)+s}, z^{\mathrm{d}}_{i+p,j+s}\right\}, p = \overline{-a, a}, s = \overline{-b, b}, \tag{3}$$

where $(x(m),\ y(m))$ are the coordinates of the point $(i,j)$ of the image $\mathbf{Z}^{\mathrm{s}}$ in the image $\mathbf{Z}^{\mathrm{d}}$ for the estimate $\hat{h}^{m}_{i,j}$ and $(2a+1)\times(2b+1)$ is the window size for calculation of CC. The optimal value $\hat{h}_{(i,j)y}$ is determined similarly.

Joint processing of estimates allows compensating the inertia of the recursive estimation. The results given below were obtained with $a = b = 1$.

The joint processing of estimates $\hat{\rho}^{l}_{i,j}$, $\hat{\rho}^{r}_{i,j}$ and $\hat{\varphi}^{l}_{i,j}$, and $\hat{\varphi}^{r}_{i,j}$ as well as finding the optimal values of $\hat{\rho}_{i,j}$ and $\hat{\varphi}_{i,j}$ are performed as described above using the same criteria of gradient estimation minimum and CC maximum.

Thus for joint processing of the estimates, depending on the criterion, we obtain two versions of the estimation algorithm:

*Algorithm A*: reverse processing using the criterion Eq. (2);

*Algorithm B*: reverse processing using the criterion Eq. (3).

## 2.2 Comparison of the estimation algorithm efficiency

Let us first consider the efficiency of the criterion Eq. (2). **Figure 2** shows an example of images used for the study. These are two adjacent frames of a video sequence where the vehicle located in the center is moving and the vehicle on the right is motionless. The parameters of inter-frame spatial shift of the moving vehicle are $h_x = 3$, $h_y = 2, 95$ or $\rho = 4, 2$, and $\varphi = 45°$.

**Figure 2.**
*An example of adjacent frames of a video sequence with a moving object.*

For example, **Figure 3** shows typical results of shift magnitude estimation for a single row of the reference image (**Figure 2**) while using Algorithm A. For a correct comparison of the estimates $\hat{\rho}_{i,j}$, $\hat{\varphi}_{i,j}$ and $\hat{h}_{(i,j)x}$, and $\hat{h}_{(i,j)y}$, the latter is recalculated to polar parameters:

$$\rho(h) = \sqrt{\left(\hat{h}_{(i,j)x}\right)^2 + \left(\hat{h}_{(i,j)y}\right)^2},\ \varphi(h) = arctg\left(\hat{h}_{(i,j)x}/\hat{h}_{(i,j)y}\right),$$

**Figure 3a** shows dependencies $\hat{\rho}^l_{i,j}$ and $\hat{\rho}^r_{i,j}$ on $i$ point in a row, **Figure 3b** shows the result of their joint processing, **Figure 3c** shows dependencies $\rho\left(h^l\right)$ and $\rho(h^r)$ on $i$, and **Figure 3d** shows the result of their joint processing. The solid gray line represents the true value of the deformation parameter. The results for parameters $(\rho, \varphi)$ are visually better. Estimates given in **Table 1** also confirm that. **Table 1** shows mean value $m_{\overline{h}}$ and variance $\hat{\sigma}^2_{\overline{h}}$ of estimation error for the area with and without motion for results shown in **Figure 3b** and **d**.

Note that with the use of parameters $(\rho, \varphi)$ in the motion area, the mean value of the estimation error is lower, and the variance is more than two times less than with the use of the set of parameters $(h_x, h_y)$. In the area without motion, the use of parameters $(\rho, \varphi)$ is also preferable since the bias of the estimates is less despite the

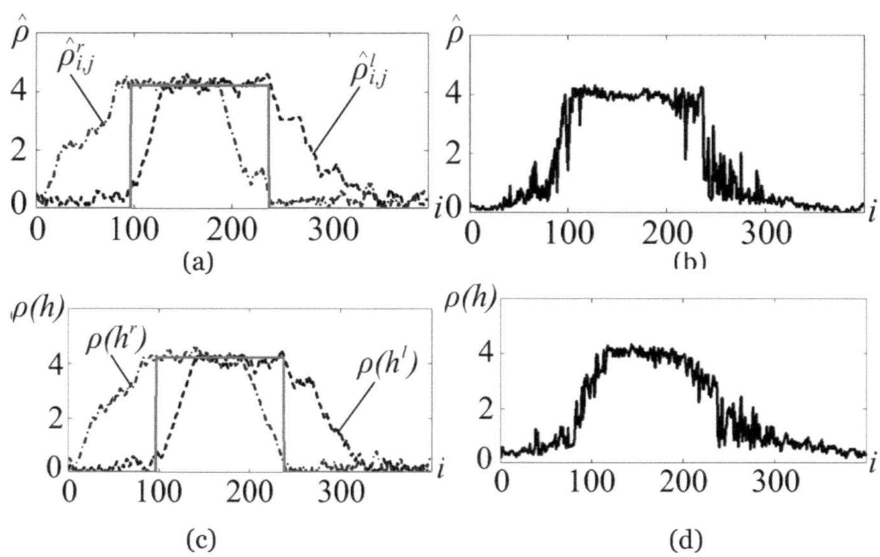


**Figure 3.**
*An example of estimates of shift magnitude for a row using criterion Eq. (2).*

| Algorithm | Motion area | | | | Area without motion | | | |
|---|---|---|---|---|---|---|---|---|
| | $m_{\overline{h}}$ | | $\hat{\sigma}^2_{\overline{h}} \times 10^{-2}$ | | $m_{\overline{h}}$ | | $\hat{\sigma}^2_{\overline{h}} \times 10^{-2}$ | |
| | $(h_x, h_y)$ | $(\rho, \varphi)$ | $(h_x, h_y)$ | $(\rho, \varphi)$ | $(h_x, h_y)$ | $(\rho, \varphi)$ | $(h_x, h_y)$ | $(\rho, \varphi)$ |
| For a single row | | | | | | | | |
| A | 0.46 | 0.31 | 21.27 | 10.41 | 0.77 | 0.49 | 21.91 | 26.11 |
| B | 0.18 | 0.1 | 11.22 | 0.66 | 0.3 | 0.15 | 3.82 | 0.89 |
| C | 0.37 | 0.06 | 19.8 | 4.84 | 0.44 | 0.22 | 3.4 | 1.42 |
| D | 0.06 | 0.01 | 0.38 | 0.26 | 0.03 | 0.02 | 0.29 | 0.03 |
| MVFAST | 0.05 | | 25.3 | | 0.01 | | 0.01 | |
| For the entire image | | | | | | | | |
| A | 0.61 | 0.53 | 23.6 | 14.3 | 0.73 | 0.45 | 23.8 | 18.8 |
| B | 0.42 | 0.34 | 7.3 | 1.7 | 0.29 | 0.15 | 2.6 | 1.5 |
| C | 0.13 | 0.14 | 15.9 | 10.1 | 0.46 | 0.25 | 2.8 | 2.9 |
| D | 0.07 | 0.01 | 1.4 | 0.69 | 0.09 | 0.02 | 0.28 | 0.02 |
| MVFAST | 0.08 | | 18.6 | | 0.02 | | 0.05 | |

**Table 1.**
*Estimation error of shift vectors of deformation field.*

slightly larger variance. For comparison, **Table 1** also shows the results for the mean value and estimation of the variance $\hat{\sigma}^2_{\overline{h}}$ of estimation errors averaged over the entire image.

**Figure 4** shows the results of the joint processing of the sets of estimates $\left(\hat{h}_{(i,j)x}, \hat{h}_{(i,j)y}\right)$ and $\left(\hat{\rho}^l_{i,j}, \hat{\rho}^r_{i,j}\right)$ using the criterion Eq. (3) of the formation of the resulting estimate (Algorithm B). The results are for the same row as the results in **Figure 3**. **Figure 4a** corresponds to the set of parameters $(h_x, h_y)$, and **Figure 4b** corresponds to $(\rho, \varphi)$. **Table 1** summarizes the numerical data of the estimation error for the row and averaging over the entire image.

The results show that the use of CC maximum as the criterion can significantly improve the results of the joint processing of the estimates. For both sets of parameters, the mean value of the error for the motion area does not exceed 0.2. The variance of the error is approximately halved for the set of parameters $(h_x, h_y)$ and 15 times less for parameters $(\rho, \varphi)$. For the area without motion, the mean error is less by about 2.6 and 3.3 times. The variance of the estimates also decreases. However, when using CC, the computational complexity of the estimation procedure increases significantly.

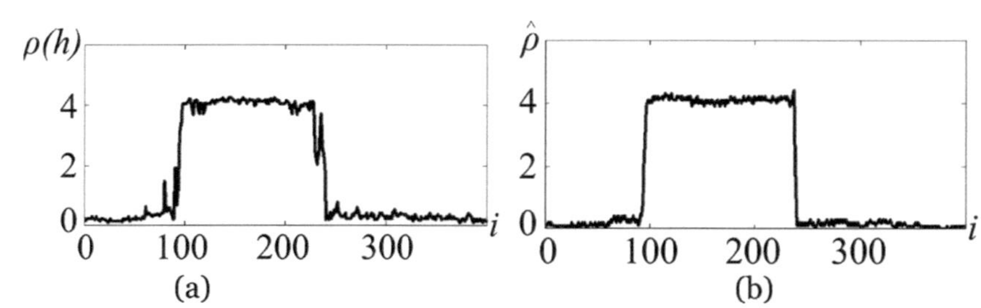


**Figure 4.**
*The resulting estimates of shift magnitude for a row using criterion Eq. (3).*

**Figure 5** shows the visualization of estimates of the shift vectors' field **H** for the four estimation algorithms described above. It shows the magnitudes of the estimated vectors as a function of coordinates of nodes of the reference image. **Figure 5a** and **b** shows the results for criteria Eqs. (2) and (3) for the set of parameters $(h_x, h_y)$ and **Figure 5c** and **d** for the same criteria when parameters $(\rho, \varphi)$ are used. The figures illustrate and confirm the conclusions made above.

### 2.3 Use of inter-row correlation of adjacent rows of the image

The approach to estimate the field **H** considered above processes images row by row as one-dimensional signals. Let us consider the possibility to increase processing efficiency by taking into account correlation of the adjacent rows of image [13, 17]. For each node $(i,j)$ of the reference image, we will also form two estimates $\hat{\overline{h}}^1_{i,j}$ and $\hat{\overline{h}}^2_{i,j}$ of the parameters of the vector $\overline{h}_{i,j}$. To form the estimate $\hat{\overline{h}}^1_{i,j}$, the stochastic gradient procedure processes rows one after the other with the change in direction after each row, for example, the odd rows from the left to the right, forming estimates $\hat{\overline{h}}^{1l}_{i,j}$, and the even rows, from the right to the left, forming estimates $\hat{\overline{h}}^{1r}_{i+1,j}$. The current shift estimate $\hat{\overline{h}}^1_{i+1,j}$ in a node is compared with the estimate $\hat{\overline{h}}^1_{i,j}$, obtained from the previous row. If the estimate $\hat{\overline{h}}^1_{i,j}$ is considered better using some criterion, then it is taken as the current estimate.

As the criterion we use CC maximum Eq. (3) with the difference that here the set of possible values is limited by the estimates $\hat{\overline{h}}^1_{i+1,j}$ and $\hat{\overline{h}}^1_{i,j}$. The estimate $\hat{\overline{h}}^2_{i,j}$ is also formed in a similar way with the difference that, when processing, the odd rows are processed from the right to the left and the even rows from the left to the right.

The joint processing of estimates $\hat{\overline{h}}^1_{i,j}$ and $\hat{\overline{h}}^2_{i,j}$ is carried out as described above. On the one hand, when taking into account inter-row correlation, the formation of $\hat{\overline{h}}^1_{i,j}$ and $\hat{\overline{h}}^2_{i,j}$ requires a greater amount of computation. On the other hand, the set of

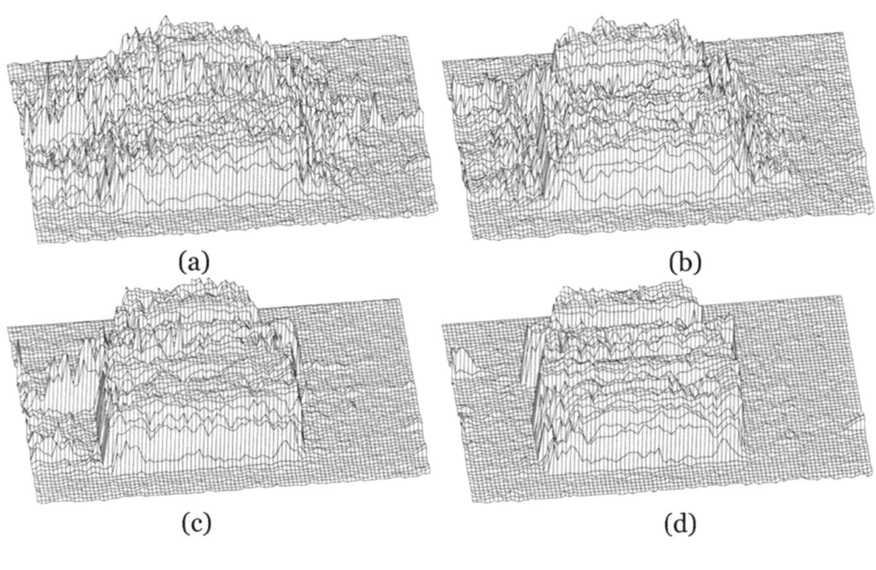

**Figure 5.**
*Visualization of estimating shift vectors' field by algorithms A and B with different criteria.*

possible estimates for their joint processing turns out to be significantly smaller, which reduces the computational complexity.

Thus we have two more algorithms to estimate the shift vectors' field:

- Algorithm C: processing of adjacent rows using the criterion Eq. (2); and
- Algorithm D: processing of adjacent rows using the criterion Eq. (3).

### 2.4 Comparison of algorithms C and D

**Figure 6** shows the typical results of joint processing of the sets of estimates $\hat{h}_{(i,j)x}, \hat{h}_{(i,j)y}$ (**Figure 6a**) and $\hat{\rho}_{i,j}$, and $\hat{\varphi}_{i,j}$ (**Figure 6b**) using Algorithm C. **Figure 6c** and **d** shows the results for the same sets and Algorithm D. It can be seen from the figures that the use of inter-row correlation can significantly improve the estimation results. For the parameters $(h_x, h_y)$ and Algorithm C, mean value of the error for motion area decreases by 1.2 times, error variance by 1.1 times, and for Algorithm D by 3 times and 29 times, respectively. For the set of parameters $(\rho, \varphi)$ and Algorithm C, the mean value of the error for motion area decreases by 5 times, variance by 2.1 times, and for Algorithm D by 10 times and 2.5 times, respectively. The numerical values are listed in **Table 1**.

**Figure 7** shows visualization of the estimates of shift vectors' field **H** for the estimation algorithms. **Figure 7a** and **b** corresponds to the algorithms C and D and set of parameters $(h_x, h_y)$, and **Figure 7c** and **d** corresponds to the same algorithms and the set of parameters $(\rho, \varphi)$. It can be seen that criterion Eq. (3) provides a greater accuracy of estimation (but also a larger computational costs). When maximum spatial accuracy is required, it is advisable to use one of algorithms B and D. The error for the Algorithm D is smaller, but the algorithm has a greater computational complexity.

**Figure 8** shows moving object area and its contour obtained from the results of algorithms C (**Figure 8a**) and D (**Figure 8b**) by thresholding with the threshold equal to 0.1 of the maximum value of shift magnitude. Note that there are practically no errors of the second kind for Algorithm D.

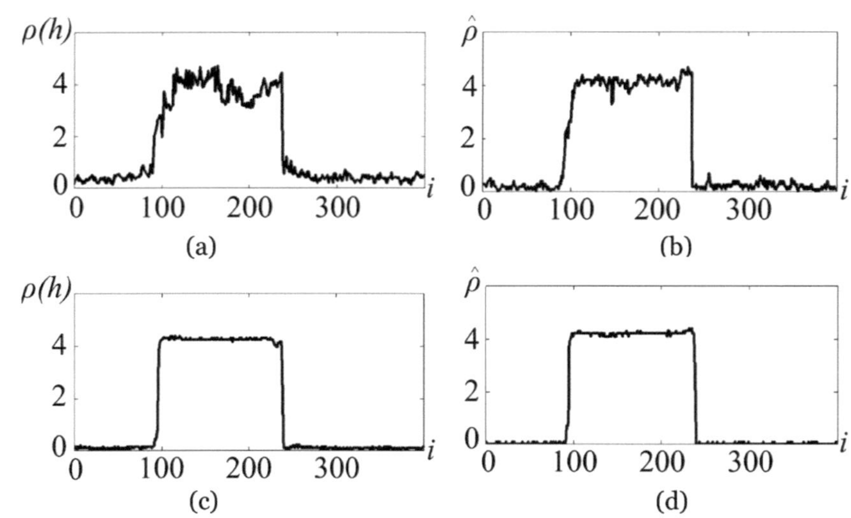


**Figure 6.**
*Example of estimates of shift magnitude for a row using inter-row correlation.*

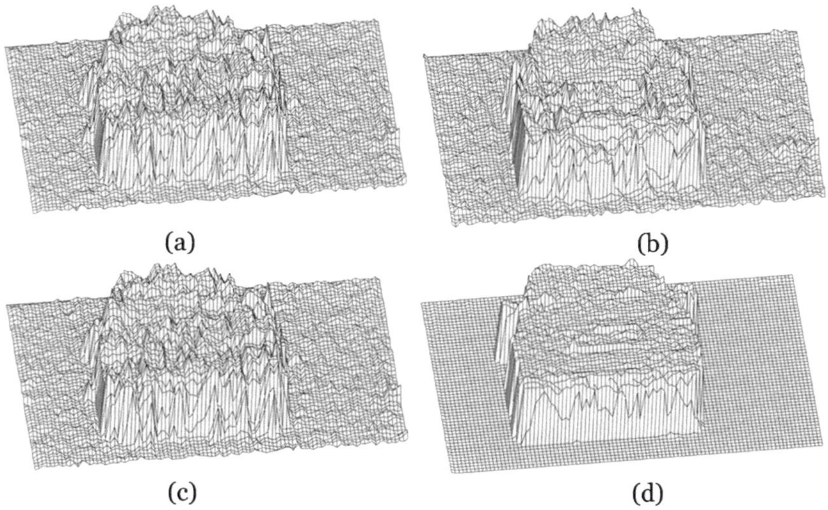


**Figure 7.**
*Visualization of shift vectors' field while using inter-row correlation.*

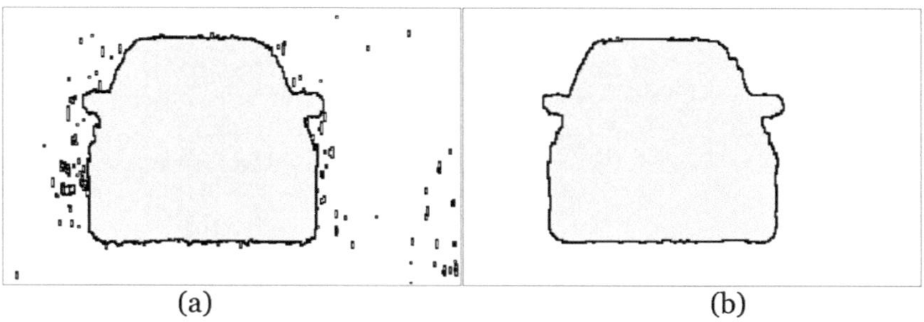


**Figure 8.**
*Results of moving object area detection.*

## 3. Efficiency of the algorithms for complex motion

Let us consider the possibilities of the developed algorithms when estimating shift vectors' field for more complex types of motion, in particular, for the case when inter-frame geometric deformations of images of a moving object can be described by a similarity model with a vector of parameters $\overline{\alpha} = (\overline{h}, \varphi, \kappa)$. To compare the results of estimation of the shift vectors' field with the results obtained for the images in **Figure 2**, the right image was modeled with the corresponding parameters of inter-frame deformations: $\overline{h} = (2, 3)^T$, $\varphi = 4°$, and $\kappa = 1$.

The results presented below are for algorithms B and D which were shown to have the highest efficiency with the use of Eq. (3) as a criterion. **Figure 9** shows typical results for a single row of the image; here graphs (a) and (b) correspond to the Algorithm B and the set of parameters $(h_x, h_y)$ and $(\rho, \varphi)$, respectively, and graphs (c) and (d) correspond to Algorithm D. In this case the estimates for the set of parameters $(\rho, \varphi)$ are closer to the true values (gray line). **Figure 10** shows visualization of estimates of the shift vectors' field for the entire image. **Figure 10a** and **b** corresponds to Algorithm B, and **Figure 10c** and **d** corresponds to Algorithm D with the set of parameters $(h_x, h_y)$ and $(\rho, \varphi)$, respectively.

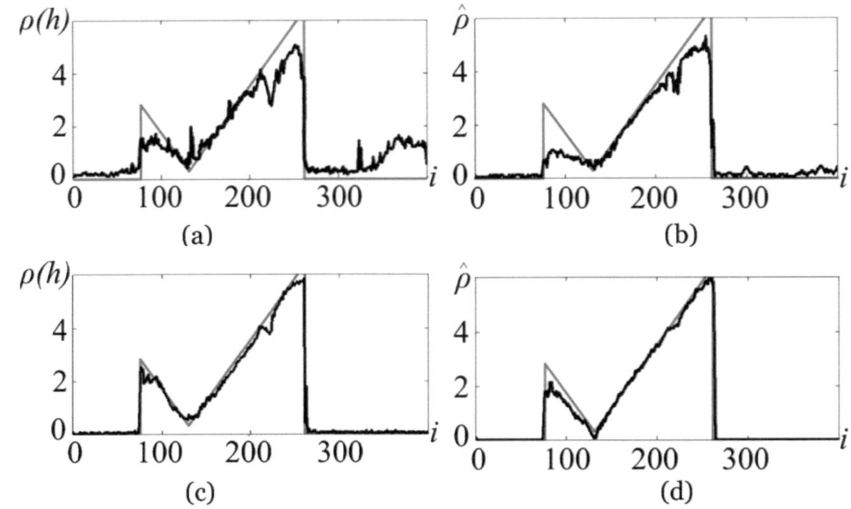


**Figure 9.**
*Example of estimates of shift magnitude for a row in case of complex motion of an object.*

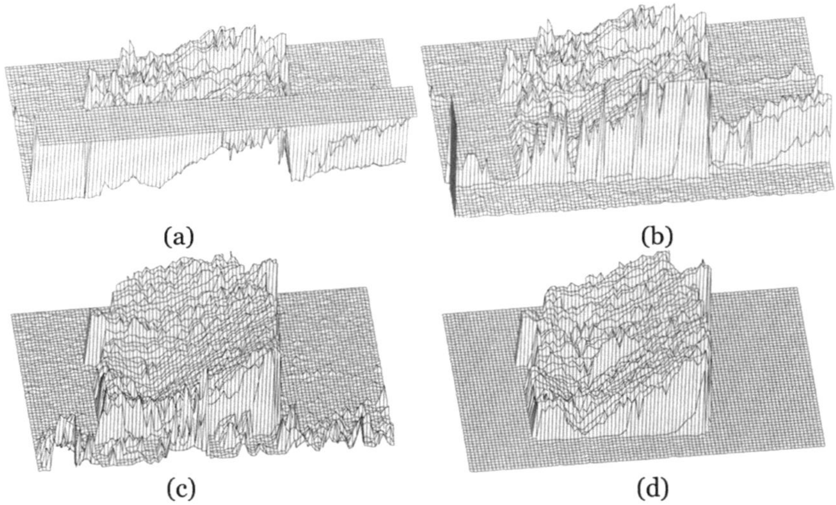


**Figure 10.**
*Visualization of shift vectors' field in case of complex motion of an object.*

In the presented figures, in order to remove outliers significantly exceeding the true value of the shift, the estimation module was limited to $\rho_{\max} = 10$. When using Algorithm B, we note a significant number of false estimates $\rho \geq \rho_{\max}$ both for and outside the area of motion. In particular, when using the parameters $(h_x, h_y)$, the estimates for a significant number of bottom rows of the image exceed the threshold. The use of the inter-row correlation significantly reduces the number of outliers for the set of parameters $(h_x, h_y)$ and virtually eliminates them for the set $(\rho, \varphi)$.

## 4. Comparison of the developed algorithms with the MVFAST algorithm

For block approach [18, 19], one of the most effective algorithms for the formation of shift vectors' field is the MVFAST (Motion Vector Field Adaptive Search

Technique) algorithm [20]. Therefore, we compare the effectiveness of the proposed algorithms and the MVFAST algorithm.

In the MVFAST algorithm, the deformed image is divided into many nonoverlapping square blocks of a predetermined size. In most cases the block sizes are $2 \times 2$, $4 \times 4$, etc., but the algorithm allows setting blocks of any size, starting from one pixel. The estimation of the shift vector for the current block is determined by the estimates of the motion vectors of the neighboring blocks. The maximum value of the motion vector length of neighboring blocks is compared with two threshold values $L_1$ and $L_2$, the values of which depend on the type of video sequence. As a result motion activity is classified as low, medium, and high. The criterion is the minimum of the sum of absolute differences (SAD). This characteristic for a block is the sum of the modules of the differences between the nodes of the current block and the corresponding nodes of the image on which the block location is searched. To improve performance and eliminate the influence of noise in the MVFAST algorithm, an early stop of the search is used. The search is terminated if the SAD is less than the specified threshold value $T$. Early stopping of the search can be disabled by setting the threshold $T$ to zero.

Let us compare the results of estimation of the deformation field by algorithms D and MVFAST. For correctness of the comparison, below are the results obtained for the images in **Figure 2** with the parameters of Algorithm D, $\lambda_h = \lambda_\rho = 0.1$, $\lambda_\varphi = \pi/180$, $\Delta x = \Delta y = 1$, $\Delta_h = \Delta_\rho = 0.2$, and $\Delta_\varphi = 5\pi/180$, and parameters of the MVFAST algorithm, $L_1 = 1$, $L_2 = 2$, $T = 1$, and block size 1x1. **Figure 11a** shows the estimates of the shift magnitude of the image points corresponding to the nodes of a single row of the reference image and formed by the MVFAST algorithm. The results of Algorithm D with the sets of parameters $(h_x, h_y)$ and $(\rho, \varphi)$ are shown in **Figure 6c** and **d**, respectively.

It can be seen from the figure that the MVFAST algorithm forms fairly accurate estimates of node shifts, but, unlike Algorithm D, it has errors at the boundaries of the image of an object. Errors also occur in low-contrast areas inside the object. The latter is due to the fact that SAD in the center of the search for them often does not exceed the threshold $T$. Setting the threshold $T = 0$ when a block size is 1 pixel also does not solve this problem. Algorithm D, due to the inertia of changes of estimates, is deprived of this disadvantage.

The values of the mathematical expectation and variance of estimation errors when using the MVFAST algorithm for a row and for the entire image are shown in **Table 1**. The table shows that the mathematical expectation of the MVFAST algorithm for the motion area is almost the same as for Algorithm D with the set of parameters $(h_x, h_y)$ but several times higher (about five times for a row, eight times for the entire image) than for Algorithm D with the set of parameters $(\rho, \varphi)$. The variance of the estimation error for the motion area for the MVFAST algorithm

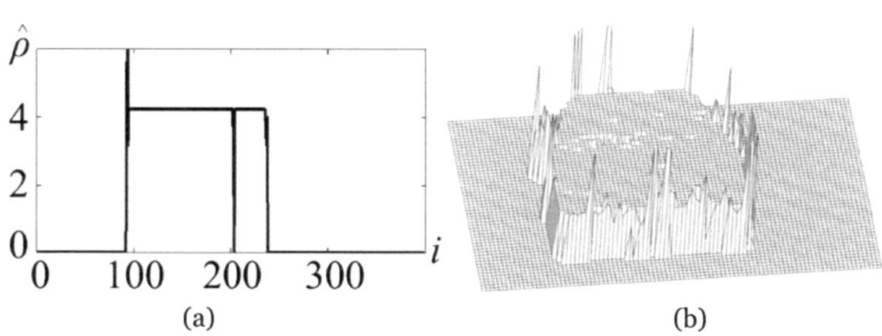


**Figure 11.**
*Example of estimates for the shift magnitude for a single row and visualization of the deformation field generated by the MVFAST algorithm.*

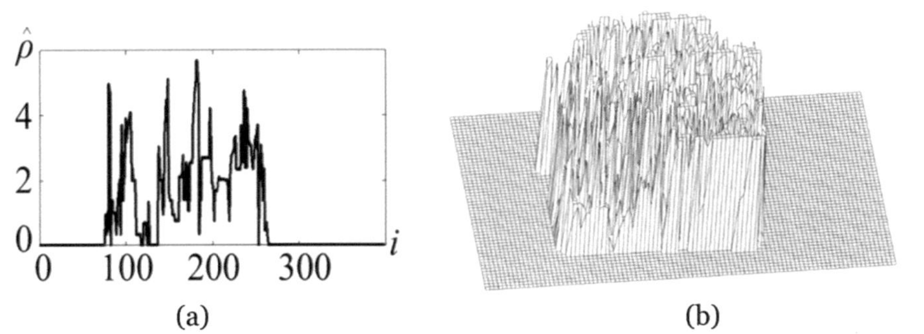


**Figure 12.**
*Example of estimates of shift magnitude for a single row and visualization of the deformation field formed by the MVFAST algorithm for complex motion.*

significantly exceeds the variance for Algorithm D (13 times with the set of parameters $(h_x, h_y)$ and 27 times with the set of parameters $(\rho, \varphi)$. In the absence of noise for area without motion, the MVFAST algorithm shows slightly better results compared to Algorithm D with the set of parameters $(h_x, h_y)$, but the results for Algorithm D with the set of parameters $(\rho, \varphi)$ is better. This is well illustrated by **Figure 11b**, which shows the visualization of the deformation field estimates for the entire image. The results of using Algorithm D with the sets of parameters $(h_x, h_y)$ and $(\rho, \varphi)$ are shown in **Figure 7b** and **d**, respectively.

Let us also compare the efficiency of the algorithms with the complex motion for the same conditions and parameters of inter-frame deformations ($\bar{h} = (2, 3)^T$, $\varphi = 4°$, $\kappa = 1$) which were used in the analysis of algorithms B and D.

**Figure 12a** shows the estimates of shift magnitudes for a single row of the reference image (the same row that was selected in the analysis of Algorithm D), when the MVFAST algorithm is used. The results of Algorithm D with the sets of parameters $(h_x, h_y)$ and $(\rho, \varphi)$ are shown in **Figure 9c** and **d**, respectively. The visualization of deformation field for the MVFAST algorithm is shown in **Figure 12b**. The deformation fields obtained by Algorithm D with the sets of parameters $(h_x, h_y)$ and $(\rho, \varphi)$ are shown in **Figure 10c** and **d**, respectively.

It can be seen from the figure that when estimating a deformation field for complex motion, the MVFAST algorithm gives significantly worse results in terms of spatial accuracy compared to the developed algorithms, and it is practically inapplicable for estimating the parameters of the motion trajectory.

Note that the increase of block size in the MVFAST algorithm allows to get rid of detection gaps inside the object image but still does not solve the problem of errors at its boundaries. At the same time, the increase of block size reduces the accuracy of moving object area detection. The proposed algorithms, in contrast to the MVFAST algorithm, provide subpixel accuracy while estimating the parameters of the shifts that is fundamentally impossible for the MVFAST algorithm.

## 5. Analysis of computational costs

Along with the accuracy of estimation, computational complexity of the algorithms is also important. In this case, the required amount of computations per pixel of the reference image with coordinates $(i,j)$ consists of two components:

- Computational cost of finding estimates $\hat{\overline{h}}^{l}_{i,j}$ and $\hat{\overline{h}}^{r}_{i,j}$ or $\hat{\rho}^{l}_{i,j}$, $\hat{\rho}^{r}_{i,j}$ and $\hat{\varphi}^{l}_{i,j}$, $\hat{\varphi}^{r}_{i,j}$;

- Computational cost of obtaining the resulting estimate in the joint processing of estimates $\hat{\overline{h}}^{l}_{i,j}$ and $\hat{\overline{h}}^{r}_{i,j}$ or a set of estimates $\hat{\rho}^{l}_{i,j}$, $\hat{\rho}^{r}_{i,j}$ and $\hat{\varphi}^{l}_{i,j}$, $\hat{\varphi}^{r}_{i,j}$.

The second component depends on many factors: complexity of the background, noise, number and speed of moving objects, etc. It can be evaluated with the given limitations of the particular problem being solved. Therefore, in the framework of this work, we restrict ourselves from analyzing the first component of computational costs with two sets of parameters for the estimated shift vectors $(h_x, h_y)$ and $(\rho, \varphi)$ for the three algorithms discussed above:

- Algorithm A: single row reverse processing

- Algorithm C: joint processing of adjacent rows using gradient estimation minimum criterion

- Algorithm D: joint processing of adjacent rows using CC maximum criterion

Detailed analysis of the computational cost requires taking into account not only algorithm itself but a large number of other factors (type of the computing device, time of memory access and for other operations, etc.). Many of these factors depend on the particular imaging device and computing resources. Therefore, we analyze only the computational complexity of the calculated ratios of the algorithms. We will consider the number of operations of addition $(+)$, subtraction $(-)$, multiplication $(\times)$, division $(\div)$, tacking the root $(\sqrt{})$, trigonometric functions $(\sin, \cos)$, and interpolations for a node $(\tilde{z})$.**Table 2** shows the number of such operations needed to process one node of an image.

The total computational cost is defined as

$$N = c_{\pm}N_{\pm} + c_{\times}N_{\times} + c_{\div}N_{\div} + c\tilde{z}N\tilde{z} + c_{\sqrt{}}N_{\sqrt{}} + c_{\sin}N_{\sin}, \quad (4)$$

| Operation | Number of operations | | | | | |
|---|---|---|---|---|---|---|
| | Algorithm A | | Algorithm C | | Algorithm D | |
| | $(h_x, h_y)$ | $(\rho, \varphi)$ | $(h_x, h_y)$ | $(\rho, \varphi)$ | $(h_x, h_y)$ | $(\rho, \varphi)$ |
| $+, -$ | 12 | 16 | 24 | 32 | 156 | 160 |
| $\times$ | 6 | 20 | 10 | 38 | 114 | 128 |
| $\div$ | — | — | — | — | 4 | 4 |
| $\tilde{z}$ | 8 | 8 | 16 | 16 | 44 | 44 |
| $\sin, \cos$ | — | 4 | — | 8 | — | 4 |
| $\sqrt{}$ | — | — | — | — | 4 | 4 |

**Table 2.**
*The number of operations needed to process a single node of an image.*

where $c_{\pm}, c_{\times}, c_{\div}, c_{\tilde{z}}, c_{\sqrt{}}, c_{\sin}$ are the coefficients characterizing the time needed to perform corresponding operations and $N_{\pm}, N_{\times}, N_{\div}, N_{\tilde{z}}, N_{\sqrt{}}, N_{\sin}$ are the number of operations.

Equation (4) allows estimating the computational cost of the algorithms for particular computing facilities. For example, for a PC with an AMD Turion II X2 M500 processor: $c_{\pm} = 1.4$, $c_{\times} = 1.4$, $c_{\div} = 13.6$, $c_{\tilde{z}} = 63$, $c_{\sqrt{}} = 135$, and $c_{\sin} = 212$ ns. Then for the set of parameters $(h_x, h_y)$, average time needed to process one node of an image is 0.53 μs for Algorithm A, 1.06 μs for Algorithm C, and 3.74 μs for Algorithm D. The average time for parameters $(\rho, \varphi)$ is 1.4 μs for Algorithm A, 2.8 μs for Algorithm C, and 4.62 μs for Algorithm D.

Let us note the features of the computational complexity of algorithms D and MVFAST. Studies have shown that the amount of computation of the latter is largely determined by the nature of the processed images. So if the adjacent frames of a video sequence do not contain motion, the computational complexity of the algorithm will be determined only by computing one SAD for each block. In the presence of motion, depending on its intensity, the computational complexity may increase in tens or even hundreds of times. In particular, when processing two frames of a video sequence without movement by the MVFAST algorithm with a block size of 1 pixel on the same PC, the average time spent on one node was 0.64 μs. This is the lowest possible computational cost. The average processing time for a single node for the images shown in **Figure 2** was 8.91 μs. For similar images with a complex type of motion, for example, with $\overline{\alpha} = \left((2,3)^T, 4°, 1\right)$, processing time is 21.84 μs. Note that the time expenses when using Algorithm D with the set of parameters $(h_x, h_y)$ were 7.44, 8.8, and 10.75 μs under similar conditions, while with the parameters $(\rho, \varphi)$, the time expenses were 8.13, 10.27, and 11.8 μs.

From the above results, it can be seen that the computational complexity of Algorithm D weakly depends on the presence or absence of moving objects, their size, and type of motion. The computational complexity of the MVFAST algorithm is largely determined by these factors. So for the case when the inter-frame deformations of images of a moving object correspond only to a parallel shift, the computation time for algorithms D and MVFAST is approximately the same. When motion is complex, it increases in several times for the MVFAST algorithm.

## 6. An example of estimating the trajectory of a moving object using deformation field

Let us give an example of estimating the trajectory of a moving object using the developed algorithms. **Figure 13a** and **b** shows two frames from the video sequence being processed in which the aircraft lands on an aircraft carrier.

A complicating factor is the uneven movement of the camera toward the landing plane. Therefore, to estimate the position of the moving object relative to the scene (not to the camera), it was necessary not only to detect and identify the moving object area but also to stabilize the image. First, the distortion caused by the movement of the camera is compensated. To do this the inter-frame deformation of adjacent frames presented as similarity model $\overline{\alpha} = (h_x, h_y, \varphi, \kappa)$ is estimated using deformation fields [21]. Then the area of a moving object is detected. Using the estimates of the deformation field in the area of moving object, the parameters of the inter-frame motion are found, which for 34 frames of the video sequence are isometrically presented in **Figure 13c**. These parameters are used to estimate a

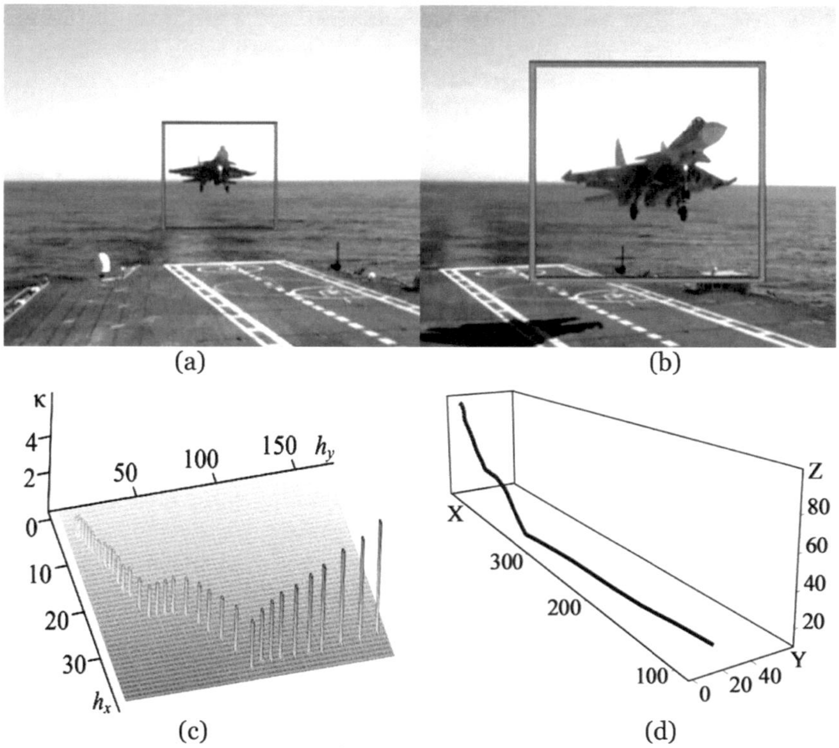


**Figure 13.**
*An example of estimation of moving object trajectory.*

three-dimensional trajectory of a moving object. **Figure 13d** shows the result in relative coordinates XYZ. The camera position at the initial moment of the shooting is taken as the origin.

## 7. Conclusion

The effectiveness of the motion area detection in sequence of images using pixel-by-pixel stochastic gradient estimation of the inter-frame shift vectors for all points of the reference image corresponding to its nodes (deformation field) is investigated. It is shown that stochastic gradient estimation of shift vectors does not give equivalent results for their representation as projections on the basic axes of the image and polar parameters. This is due to the fact that these sets of parameters have a different physical meaning. The analysis of variants of estimation algorithms for the deformation field has shown that the use of polar parameters provides higher accuracy of estimation.

Two approaches to estimate the parameters of the deformation field are considered. In the first approach, the stochastic gradient procedure sequentially processes all rows of an image to find estimates of shifts for all points of the reference image. It processes each row bidirectionally, i.e., from the left to the right and from the right to the left. The joint processing of the results allows compensating the inertia of the stochastic estimation. However, this approach does not take into account inter-row correlation, and images are processed as one-dimensional signals. In the second approach, to improve the accuracy of estimation, the correlation of image rows is taken into account. Algorithm processes rows one after the other with change in direction after each row and uses obtained values to form resulting estimate for each node. From the results obtained for each node of the reference image, the resulting estimate of the shift vector is formed. Studies have shown that the second approach, with approximately the same computational complexity, showed significantly higher accuracy in the estimation of the shift vectors' field.

As a criterion for the formation of the resulting estimate, the minimum of gradient estimation of the objective function and the correlation maximum of local neighborhoods of the deformed and reference images were investigated. Correlation maximum criterion showed the best results. When using this criterion, not only the mean value and the variance of the estimation errors turned out to be less but also the effect of "oscillations" outside the motion area. But the use of this criterion requires a large computational cost.

The computational complexity of the proposed algorithms is investigated. Under equal conditions, the estimation of the projections of the shift vectors requires a slightly smaller amount of computations than the estimation of polar parameters. Using reverse processing of a row is less time-consuming compared with processing of the adjacent rows. The use of the correlation maximum criterion implies a larger amount of calculations than the use of the gradient estimation minimum criterion. The algorithms with large computational costs provide less error; therefore the choice of algorithm depends on the specific task.

The experiments have confirmed the effectiveness of using the developed algorithms to find the motion parameters and the trajectories of objects in a video sequence. In particular, an example of estimating three-dimensional trajectory of an aircraft in relative coordinates using 34 frames of a video sequence is considered. The parameters of the similarity model (parallel shift, rotation angle, and scale factor) were used to describe the inter-frame motion.

Comparison of the developed algorithms with the block algorithm MVFAST (Motion Vector Field Adaptive Search Technique) showed that under identical conditions, the latter shows worse results in accuracy of detecting the boundaries of motion. In addition, in contrast to the MVFAST algorithm, the proposed algorithms allow obtaining subpixel estimation accuracy.

Thus, the conducted study allows us to conclude that the pixel-by-pixel interframe estimation of the shift vectors of the reference image points corresponding to its nodes is a promising approach in detecting the area of a moving object in a series of images.

## Acknowledgements

The reported study was funded by the RFBR and Government of Ulyanovsk Region according to the research projects 18-41-730006 and 18-41-730011.

**Author details**

Alexander Tashlinskii[1] and Pavel Smirnov[2]*

1 Ulyanovsk State Technical University, Ulyanovsk, Russia

2 Ulyanovsk Instrument Manufacturing Design Bureau, Ulyanovsk, Russia

*Address all correspondence to: rtcis@mail.ru

## References

[1] Elhabian SY, El-Sayed KM, Ahmed SH. Moving object detection in spatial domain using background removal techniques. Recent Patents on Computer Science. 2008;**1**(1):32-54. DOI: 10.2174/1874479610801010032

[2] Karasulu B, Korukoglu S. Moving object detection and tracking in videos. In: Performance Evaluation Software. Springer Briefs in Computer Science. USA, New York, NY : Springer, 2013. pp. 7-30. DOI: 10.1007/11612704_16

[3] Wang L, Yung NHC. Extraction of moving objects from their background based on multiple adaptive threshold and boundary evaluation. IEEE Transactions on Intelligent Transportation Systems. 2010;**1**(11): 40-51. DOI: 10.1109/TITS.2009.2026674

[4] Kutsov RV, Trifonov AP. Detection of a moving object in the image. Journal of Computer and Systems Sciences International. 2006;**3**(45):459-468. DOI: 10.1134/S1064230706030129

[5] Grishin SV, Vatolin DS, Lukin AS. The block methods review of motion estimation in digital video signals. Programmnye Sistemy i Instrumenty. 2008;**1**(9):50-62. [in Russian]

[6] Zolotykh NY, Kustikova VD, Meerov IB. The review of searching and tracking methods in video. Vestnik Nizhegorodskogo universiteta im N.I. Lobachevskogo. 2012;**5**(2):348-358. [in Russian]

[7] Tsypkin YZ. Information Theory of Identification. Moscow: Fizmatlit; 1995. 336 p. [in Russian]

[8] Tashlinskii AG. Computational expenditure reduction in pseudo-gradient image parameter estimation. Lecture Notes in Computer Science. 2003;**2658**:456-462. DOI: 10.1007/3-540-44862-4_48

[9] Tashlinskii AG. Pseudogradient estimation of digital images interframe geometrical deformations. In: Obinata G, Dutta A, editors. Vision Systems: Segmentation & Pattern Recognition. Austria, Vienna: I-Tech; 2007. pp. 465-494. DOI: 10.5772/4975

[10] Tashlinskii AG. Optimization of goal function pseudogradient in the problem of interframe geometrical deformations estimation. In: Yin PY, editor. Pattern Recognition Techniques, Technology and Applications. Austria, Vienna: I-Tech; 2008. pp. 249-280. DOI: 10.5772/6244

[11] Tashlinskii AG, Smirnov PV, Biktimirov LS. Methods of finding gradient estimates of target function for measurement of images parameters. Pattern Recognition and Image Analysis. 2011;**2**(21):339-342. DOI: 10.1134/S1054661811021057

[12] Tashlinskii AG, Khoreva AM, Smirnov PV. Selection of finite differences in finding the stochastic gradient of the objective function in the estimation procedures of interframe deformations of images. Radiotekhnika. 2012;**9**:56-60. [in Russian]

[13] Smirnov PV, Tashlinskii AG. Method for moving object area identification in image sequence. Radiotekhnika. 2015;**6**:5-11. [in Russian]

[14] Tashlinskii AG, Kurbanaliev RM, Zhukov SS. Method for detecting instability and recovery of signal shape under intense noise. Pattern Recognition and Image Analysis. 2013; **3**(23):425-428. DOI: 10.1134/S1054661813030139

[15] Tashlinskii AG, Smirnov PV, Tsaryov MG. Pixel-by-pixel estimation of scene motion in video. International Archives of the Photogrammetry. Remote Sensing and Spatial

Information. 2017;**XLII-2/W4**:61-65. DOI: 10.5194/isprs-archives-XLII-2-W4-61-2017

[16] Tashlinskii AG, Smirnov PV. Pixel-by-pixel estimation of interframe geometric deformations of images in case selecting the area of a moving object. Avtomotizatsiia Protsessov Upravleniia. 2015;**1**(39):41-49. [in Russian]

[17] Tashlinskii AG, Smirnov PV. Moving object area identification in image sequence. In: International Siberian Conference on Control and Communications (SIBCON); 21–23 May 2015; Russia. Omsk: IEEE; 2015. pp. 1-5. DOI: 10.1109/SIBCON.2015.7147239

[18] Bogush RP, Lysenko VI, Samoschenkov GA. Blocks-based algorithms combination for optical flow calculation for moving objects detection and tracking in video sequences. Vestnik Polotskogo Gosudarstvennogo Universiteta. Fundamentalnye Nauki. 2011;**4**:2-7. [in Russian]

[19] Grishin SV, Vatolin DS, Lukin AS. Review of block methods of motion estimation in digital video signals. Programmnye Sistemy i Instrumenty. 2008;**9**:50-62. [in Russian]

[20] Hosur PI, Ma KK. Motion vector field adaptive fast motion estimation. In: Second International Conference on Information, Communications and Signal Processing (ICICS 1999); December 1999; Singapore. pp. 7-10

[21] Kaveev IN, Tashlinskii AG. Estimate parameters of the affine model of image binding by conjugate points. In: Negoda VN, editor. Informatika, Modelirovanie, Avtomatizatsiia: Sbornik Nauchnykh Trudov. Ulyanovsk: UlSTU; 2009. pp. 109-111. [in Russian]

Chapter 3

# Depth Extraction from a Single Image and Its Application

*Shih-Shuo Tung and Wen-Liang Hwang*

## Abstract

In this chapter, a method for the generation of depth map was presented. To generate the depth map from an image, the proposed approach involves application of a sequence of blurring and deblurring operations on a point to determine the depth of the point. The proposed method makes no assumptions with regard to the properties of the scene in resolving depth ambiguity in complex images. Since applications involving depth map manipulation can be achieved by obtaining all-in-focus images through a deblurring operation and then blurring the obtained images, we have presented methods to derive all-in-focus images from our depth maps. Furthermore, 2D to 3D conversion can also be achieved from the estimated depth map. Some demonstrations show the performance and applications of the estimated depth map in this chapter.

**Keywords:** depth estimation, blur estimation, depth from defocus, all in focus, refocusing, defocus magnification, 2D to 3D

## 1. Introduction

Derivation of depth information from 2D images is one of the most important issues in the field of image processing and computer vision. The depth information can be applied in 2D to 3D conversion, image refocusing, scene interpretation, the reconstruction of 3D scenes, and depth-based image editing. There are some techniques used to derive depth information, such as depth from focus [1], stereo vision [2], and depth from motion [3]. Nevertheless, these techniques are complicated by the need to acquire multiple images, thereby making them impractical when only one image is available or the features corresponding between the images cannot be resolved well. To this end, a number of approaches have been proposed to acquire depth information from a single image, such as the computational photography approach [4], which modifies the shape of the aperture of a traditional lens, and the Kinect approach [5], which uses a structured light to derive depth maps.

An image captured by a conventional camera contains a blurred version of a scene that is out of focus. The blurriness of a pixel is called the "circle of confusion" (COC) and is usually modeled as a 2D Gaussian function. When a single image is taken by a conventional camera with a fixed focal length, aperture size, and distance from the image plane to the lens, a pixel's COC is related only to the depth of the corresponding scene point. In such cases, depth estimation corresponds to blur estimation. Theoretically, if the depth map of an image can be accurately estimated, applications that manipulate depths of objects can be run by first applying deblurring followed by blurring operations. This is because the deblurring operation will move the objects closer and the blurring operation will move them farther away from the camera.

Blurring operation is more robust to depth map inaccuracy than the deblurring one, and many applications have been successfully built based on this operation. For example, defocus magnification [6] increases the out-of-focus area in an image by magnifying the existing blurriness to keep the shape of sharp regions and by modifying the depths of objects that are not in the focal plane to move the objects farther away from the plane. Deblurring operation, on the other hand, can be very sensitive to the accuracy of a depth map. A deblurring operation usually highlights the edged and textured points in an image. If their depths are overestimated, the operation can generate ringing artifacts that severely degrade the perceptual quality of an image.

The depth map estimation from an image is a fundamentally ill-posed problem. For example, in a single image, we cannot resolve the ambiguity between out-of-focus edges and the original smooth edges, we cannot determine whether blurriness of a point is in the front of focal plane or behind the focal plane, and we cannot estimate the depths of points in a smooth area. These problems cannot be resolved without the assumptions between the local image features and the scene. In this context, a widely adopted assumption is that a blurred edge is obtained via smoothing a step edge with a Gaussian kernel [7]. Although this assumption has been adopted in an autofocus system of a camera, the goal of the autofocus is to derive the depths of manually selected scene points rather than the depth map of an image. The approach that is based on the assumption on scene points has also been used in estimating a depth map. Edges in a scene are first modeled, and the depths of the blurred edge points are then derived from the degree of blurriness that has been applied on the scene to obtain the points. However, because many types of

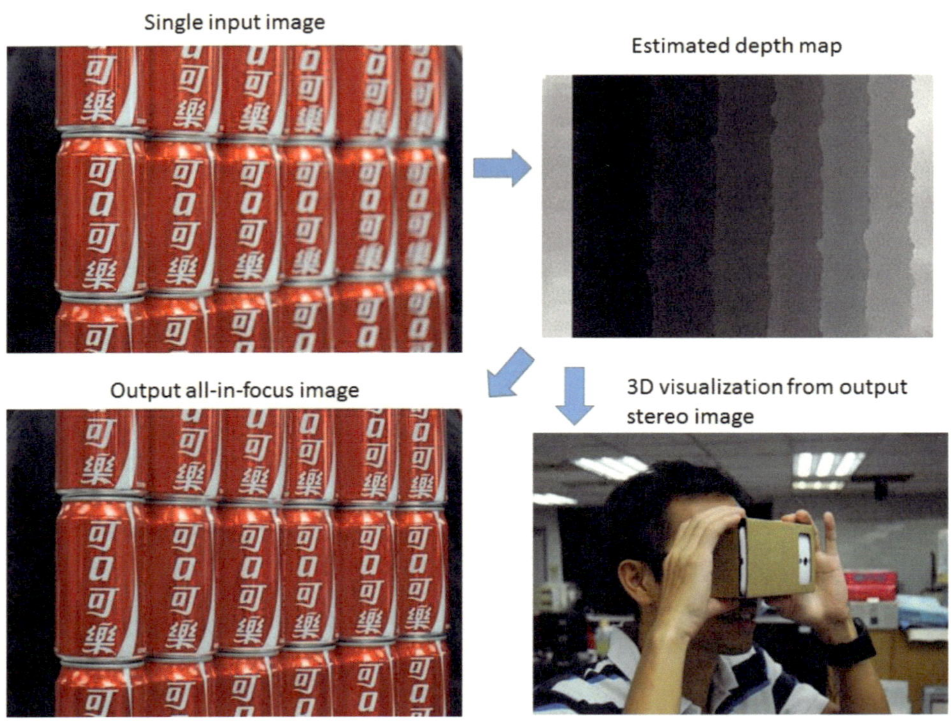


**Figure 1.**
*Applications from the depth map of a single image.*

singularities far beyond the step edges in the scene can appear in an image, the approach based on the scene modeling can be too restricted, as only a few types of singularities can be modeled, to derive precise depths of all points. As a result, the depth precision derived based on scene modeling is usually limited to images with two depth layers, foreground and background.

In this chapter, we propose a blurring-deblurring method that does not require the modeling of edge points. In the blurring process, a point is blurred by increasing its COC to the limit of a camera. However, in the deblurring process, a point is deblurred by reducing its COC to the limit in the other end. Combine the results of these two processes and derive the depths of edges. Therefore, the approach estimates the depths of edge points based on the characteristic curve of COC vs. the depth characteristic curve of a camera. We demonstrated that the proposed approaches can reliably derive depth maps of complex images and synthesize all-in-focus images. Furthermore, the depth maps can also be applied to synthesize the stereo image to 3D visualization through the mobile device. **Figure 1** shows a diagram of applications from the depth map of a single image.

The remainder of this chapter is organized as the following. The relationship between the depth of a point and out-of-focus blurriness in images obtained by the thin-lens camera model is reviewed in Section 2. The proposed blurring-deblurring approach is presented in Section 3. The depth refinement approach and image deblurring process are presented in Section 4. In Section 5, we demonstrated the depth map results and applications. Section 6 contains some conclusions.

## 2. Camera model and out-of-focus blurriness

The out-of-focus blurriness is defined by the COC if an object is not in the camera's focal plane. However, it is impossible to determine whether an object is behind or in front of the focal plane based on the blurriness of an object [8]. In the following, we consider a case of the condition.

In a thin-lens model,

$$\frac{1}{u}+\frac{1}{v}=\frac{1}{f}, \tag{1}$$

where $u$ is the distance between the lens and the scene point, $v$ is the distance between the focal plane and the lens, and $f$ is the focal length of the lens. If a light point is not in the focal plane but placed in front of the camera, the source's image will be a circular disk with diameter $D_{COC}$ instead of a point, as shown in **Figure 2**. Let $d$ be the distance between the lens and the image sensor. Then, the in-focus scene distance $u_{in-focus}$ can be derived as follows:

$$\frac{1}{u_{in-focus}}+\frac{1}{v}=\frac{1}{f}. \tag{2}$$

For a particular lens, the focal length $f$ and the aperture $A$ are constants; the F-number $N=\frac{f}{A}$ is also a constant. Given the geometric relationship $D_{COC}(u)$ shown in **Figure 2** and the lens formula, the COC's diameter of a scene point at distance $u$ from the lens depends on whether $u > u_{in-focus}$ (the scene point is farther from the lens than the focal plane) or $u < u_{in-focus}$ (the scene point is closer to the lens than the focal plane).

In the case where $u > u_{in-focus}$, we can derive the following relationship from the similar triangles shown in **Figure 2(a)**:

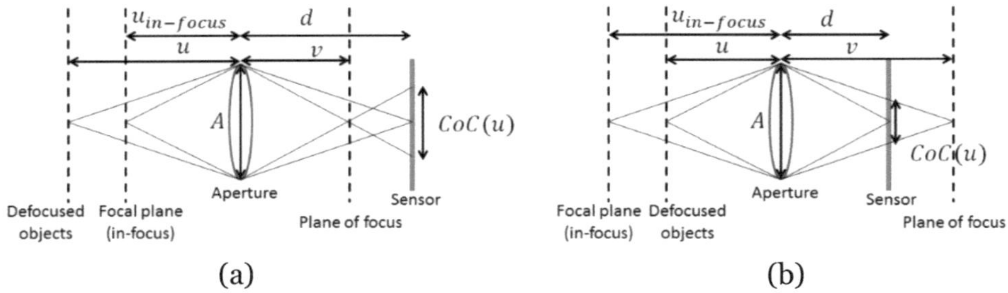


**Figure 2.**
*The geometry of imaging:* u *is the distance of a scene point from the lens,* $u_{in-focus}$ *is the distance of the focal plane from the lens,* d *is the distance between the lens and the image sensor, and the diameter of the lens' aperture is* A. *(a)* $u > u_{in-focus}$ *and (b)* $u < u_{in-focus}$.

$$\frac{D_{COC}(u)}{A} = \frac{d-v}{v}. \tag{3}$$

Using Eq. (1) and $N = \frac{f}{A}$, we obtain

$$D_{COC}(u) = \left(-1 + \frac{d}{f} - \frac{d}{u}\right)\frac{f}{N}. \tag{4}$$

In the case where $u < u_{in-focus}$, we can derive the following relationship from similar triangles shown in **Figure 2(b)**:

$$\frac{D_{COC}(u)}{A} = \frac{v-d}{v}. \tag{5}$$

Using Eq. (1) and $N = \frac{f}{A}$, we obtain

$$D_{COC}(u) = \left(1 - \frac{d}{f} + \frac{d}{u}\right)\frac{f}{N}. \tag{6}$$

From Eqs. (4) and (6), we can derive $D_{COC}$ of a scene point; however, the equations do not allow us to determine whether the scene point is in front of or behind the focal plane. To remove the ambiguity, the assumption that all the scene points are behind the focal plane is adopted.

An image is usually modeled as the convolution of the scene and a camera-relative PSF. The Pillbox function is an ideal PSF, which is a box function with support σ and constant value $\frac{1}{\sigma}$. Usually, the Gaussian function is the approximation of the Pillbox function, and the standard derivation of the Gaussian function is $\frac{\sigma}{\sqrt{2}}$. Due to the factor, the difference between their frequency domain magnitudes is small, and the latter is easier to do analysis. In this chapter, we will use the Gaussian function to characterize the PSF of a camera.

## 3. Blurring and deblurring approach

Using the proposed approach, scene depths will be determined from the estimated blurriness in a single image by using a combination of blurring and deblurring processes. In this section, we will explain the rationale for combining the blurring and deblurring processes and provide the formulation of the combined approach. The depth of a scene point is defined as the distance between the camera lens and the point. In addition, the proposed method assumes that all the interested scene points are behind the focal plane (it matches to the case: $u > u_{in-focus}$) as [9].

### 3.1 Concept

The ($D_{COC}$ vs. $u$) curve of Eq. (4), illustrated in **Figure 3(a)**, gives the relationship between the depth of a scene point and its $D_{COC}$ value of a camera. The latter increases with the depth of the scene point. When $D_{COC}$ reaches its limit ($D^*_{COC}$), the point can be assumed to be at infinity.

Let $D_{COC}$ be the blurriness of a point. A blurring operator can be defined to add an increment of blurriness to the point to obtain a new blurriness $D_{COC} + \delta(D_{COC})$, with $\delta(D_{COC}) > 0$. This can be regarded as increasing the depth of the point by moving it along the ($D_{COC}$ vs. $u$) curve toward the right end point of the figure. If the blurring operation is applied repeatedly, the blurriness can reach $D^*_{COC}$ and the point is at infinity.

If the increment in the blurriness of a point to reach $D^*_{COC}$ can be determined, we can convert this increment into the increment in depth by referring to the curve ($D_{COC}$ vs. $u$) in **Figure 3(a)** and derive the true depth of the point. However, as shown in the curve $\frac{\partial u}{\partial D_{COC}}$ of **Figure 3(b)**, a small increment in blurriness close to $D^*_{COC}$ yields a substantially large increment of depth. This means that the depth determination close to $D^*_{COC}$ is relatively unstable and inaccurate.

On the other hand, the deblurring operator is defined to reduce the blurriness of the point to obtain $D_{COC} - \delta(D_{COC})$. If a deblurring operation is repeatedly applied to a point, the latter will become sharper. The deblurring process gradually reduces the depth of the point by moving it along the ($D_{COC}$ vs. $u$) curve toward the left end point, corresponding to move the point to the focal plane or be in focus. If the decrement in blurriness, by making a point in-focus, can be determined, we can convert the decrement to the decrement in depth of the point to the focal plane. Then, we refer to the curve ($D_{COC}$ vs. $u$) in **Figure 3(a)** to acquire the true depth of the point. However, as shown in the curve $\frac{\partial u}{\partial D_{COC}}$ of **Figure 3(b)**, a small decrement

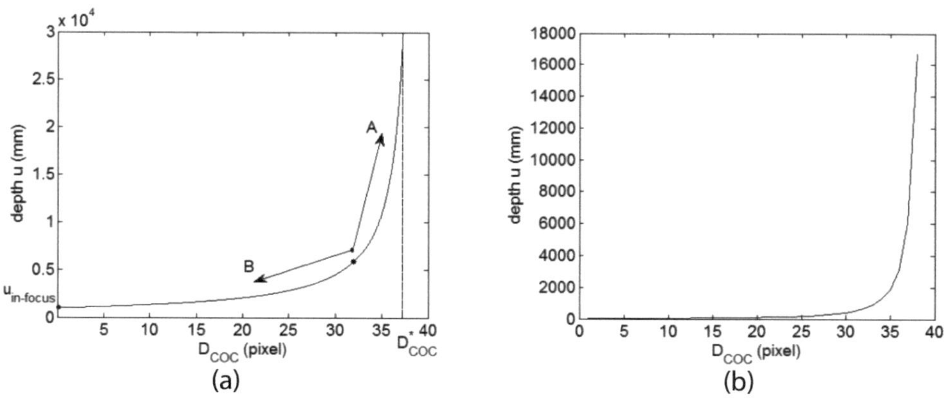


**Figure 3.**
*The relation between the out-of-focus blurriness and the distance u in Eq. (4) in the pixel domain, where $u_{in-focus}$ = 1000 mm, f = 50 mm, N = 5.6, d = 52.6316 mm, 0.0061 mm per pixel, and $D^*_{COC}$ is 38.5184. (a) Plot of $D_{COC}$ versus u, the depth. The limit of $D_{COC}$ is denoted by $D^*_{COC}$. In the blurring process, the dotted point is moved along curve A. In the deblurring process, the point is moved along curve B. (b) The derivation of curve (a). When u approaches , the blurring process fails to estimate the depth. When u is close to the focal plane, $u_{in-focused}$, the deblurring process fails in the area.*

in depth close to the focal plane can yield a substantial decrement in $D_{COC}$, which means that $D_{COC}$ cannot be reliably and accurately obtained when the point moves closer to the focal plane by a deblurring operation.

Since the depth estimation at large $D_{COC}$ and the $D_{COC}$ estimation of a point close to focal plane are unreliable, we were motivated to propose the blurring and deblurring approach that combines the differential blurring and deblurring operations to yield a more robust depth estimation of a scene point than only using one of them.

### 3.2 Formulation

Let $u_0$ be the true depth of the point at $x$; and let $F_b(x, u - u_0 + u_\infty)$ and $F_d(x, u - u_0 + u_{in-focused})$ be the blurring measurement and deblurring measurement, respectively. The blurring measurement measures whether a point is blurred to $D^*_{COC}$, and the deblurring measurement measures whether that point is deblurred to be in-focus. We define that $F_b(x, u - u_0 + u_\infty)$ is a proper function with a (local) minimum near $u_\infty$ and $F_d(x, u - u_0 + u_{in-focused})$ is a proper function with a (local) minimum near $u_{in-focused}$. The following formula is used to determine the true depth $u_0$ of the point $x$:

$$\min_u \lambda F_b(x, u - u_0 + u_\infty) + F_d(x, u - u_0 + u_{in-focused}), \tag{7}$$

with the constraint that

$$\Delta D^b_{COC}(u) + \Delta D^d_{COC}(u) = D^*_{COC} - D_{COC}(u_{in-focused}), \tag{8}$$

where $D^*_{COC} - D_{COC}(u_{in-focused})$ is a camera-dependent constant and $\lambda$ is the Lagrangian parameter that balances the blurriness and deblurriness measurements, and

$$\Delta D^b_{COC}(u) = D^*_{COC} - D_{COC}(u) \tag{9}$$

is the increment of blurriness to $D^*_{COC}$ and

$$\Delta D^d_{COC}(u) = D_{COC}(u) - D_{COC}(u_{in-focused}) \tag{10}$$

denotes the decrement of the $D_{COC}$ assuming the point at depth $u$ to the focal plane. The constraint in Eq. (8) is necessary because it indicates that the sum of the added blurriness from the current guess $u$ to $D^*_{COC}$ and the reduced blurriness from $u$ to $D_{COC}(u_{in-focused})$ is a constant, $D^*_{COC} - D_{COC}(u_{in-focused})$.

### 3.3 Blurring and deblurring measurements

For a simplified analysis but without any loss of generality, the following derivations were based on one-dimensional signals and neglecting the boundary conditions.

#### *3.3.1. Blurring measurement*

The objective of the blurring process is to determine the amount of blurriness required for a point to reach $D^*_{COC}$. When edged or textured patches are gradually placed at far distance, the details of the patches become faint, their variances decrease, and only their mean brightness can be derived at infinity. Thus, the variance of a patch can be used as the blurriness measurement. Specifically, when a patch is blurred to reach $D^*_{COC}$, its variance can be assumed to be 0.

Let the true depth of the scene point $x$ be $u_0$, and let the image of the point be

$$f_0(x) = g\left(\sigma(u_0)^2\right) * s(x) \tag{11}$$

where g is the Gaussian function and $\sigma(u_0)^2$ is the variance of $g$ at depth $u_0$. We define the blurriness measurement as follows:

$$F_b(x, u - u_0 + u_\infty) = \left\| g\left(\sigma(u_\infty)^2 - \sigma(u)^2\right) * f_0(u) - E\{f_0(x)\} \right\|^2, \tag{12}$$

where $E\{f_0(x)\}$ is the mean on a neighborhood of $f_0(x)$ and $\sigma(u_\infty) = D^*_{COC}$. Assuming that $\sigma_b^2 = \sigma(u_\infty)^2 - \sigma(u)^2$, we obtain from Eqs. (11) and (12)

$$\left\| g(\sigma_b^2) * f_0(x) - E\{f_0(x)\} \right\|^2 = \left\| g\left(\sigma_b^2 + \sigma(u_0)^2\right) * s(x) - E\{f_0(x)\} \right\|^2. \tag{13}$$

The above equation is derived by using the fact that the convolution of two Gaussians of variances $\sigma_1^2$ and $\sigma_2^2$ is a Gaussian of variance $\sigma_1^2 + \sigma_2^2$. If u is equal to $u_0$, then $\sigma_b^2 + \sigma(u_0)^2 = \sigma(u_\infty)^2$ and it becomes

$$\left\| g\left(\sigma(u_\infty)^2\right) * s(x) - E\{f_0(x)\} \right\|^2 \approx 0, \tag{14}$$

since $g\left(\sigma(u_\infty)^2\right) * s(x)$ can be approximated as the mean of $f_0(x)$. Thus, $F_b(x, u - u_0 + u_\infty)$ reaches a local minimum when u is equal to $u_0$.

### *3.3.2 Deblurring measurement using blurring-deblurring operator*

In contrast to blurring, deblurring is extremely unstable, and it usually assumes some prior knowledge of the scene so that the high-frequency (edge and texture) information can be recovered. Because of the prior assumption, when the estimated depth is overestimated, ringing artifact occurs in the result of the deblurring process.

We denote $g\left(\sigma(u)^2\right) * g^{-1}\left(\sigma(u)^2\right)$ as the blurring-deblurring operator, where $g^{-1}\left(\sigma(u)^2\right)$ is the reduction in blurriness of a Gaussian kernel with variance $\sigma(u)^2$. An image is first deblurred and then blurred by the same Gaussian kernel with variance $\sigma(u)^2$. A deblurring process will tend to over-enhance the high-frequency information in the image if $u$ is an overestimated depth. As shown by the subfigures in the second row of **Figure 4(c)**, it causes severe artifacts. So, the measurement of the error from the blurring-deblurring operator of a given point is proposed in the following:

$$S(x, u) = \left\| f_0(x) - g\left(\sigma(u)^2\right) * g^{-1}\left(\sigma(u)^2\right) * f_0(x) \right\|^2. \tag{15}$$

As shown in **Figure 4(d)**, when the estimation of the blurring scale is over the true scale (the scale is 4), the result of $S(x, u)$ increases dramatically because of the artifacts in the neighborhood of the edge points.

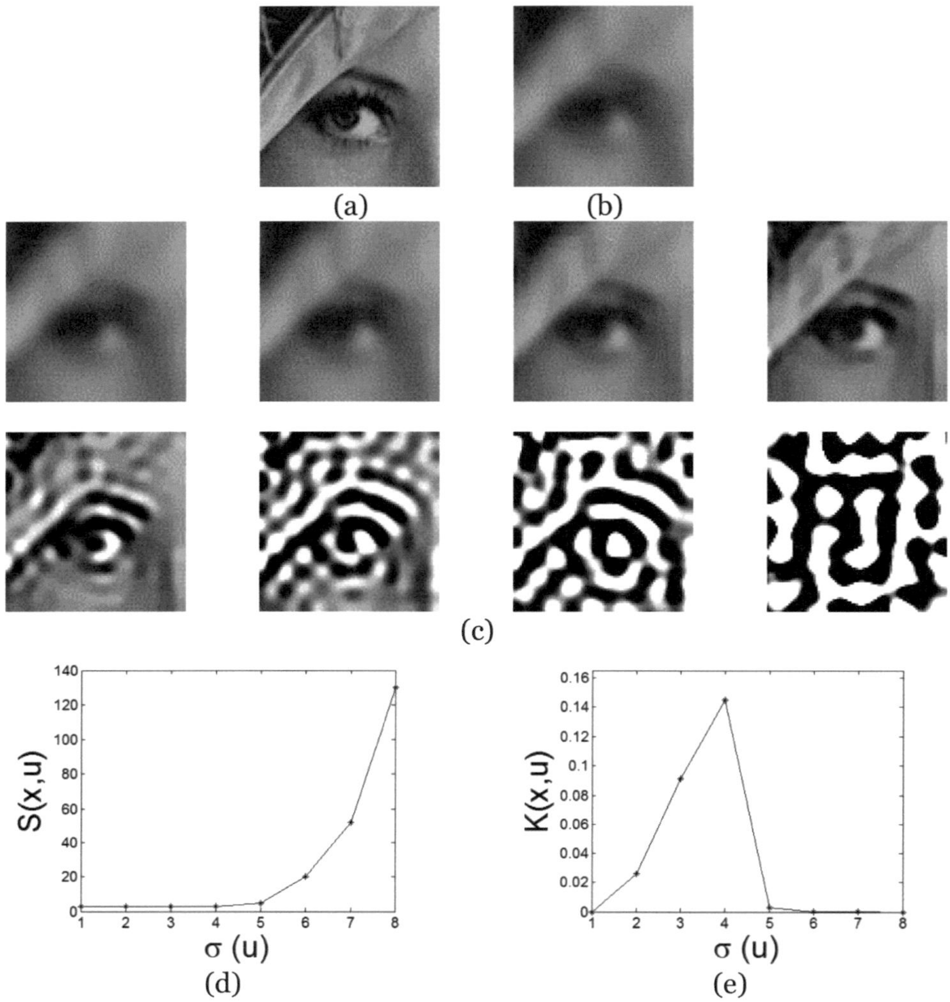


**Figure 4.**
*(a) The patch was taken from the eye of the "Lena" image, (b) the blurred patch of (a) with blurring scale 4, (c) the candidate scene patches obtained by deblurring the patch in (b) with a TV-based method (section 4.3) and different blurring scales whose standard deviations ranged from 1 to 8, and (d) the curve of* $S(x, u_j)$ *and (e)* $K(x, u_j)$*, with* $j = 1, \cdots, 8$.

From **Figure 4(d)**, $S(x, u)$ is asymmetric with respect to over- and underestimation of $u_0$, where $u_0$ is the true blurring scale or true depth. To capture the transition point from small to large values of $S(x, u)$, we calculated the curvature at $u_j$ of the smooth curve as follows:

$$K(x, u_j) = \frac{S(x, u_{j+1}) - 2S(x, u_j) + S(x, u_{j-1})}{\left(1 + \left(S(x, u_{j+1}) - S(x, u_j)\right)^2\right)^{1.5}}, \tag{16}$$

as shown in **Figure 4(e)**. The larger the value of the curvature, higher is the probability that it is the pivot point for the transition. Thus, we define the deblurring measurement as follows:

$$F_d(x, u - u_0 + u_{in-focused}) = -K(x, u). \tag{17}$$

The measure $F_d(x, u - u_0 + u_{in-focused})$ has a local minimum at the transition of $S(x, u)$. Thus, when $u$ is equal to $u_0$, $F_d(x, u - u_0 + u_{in-focused})$ becomes the minimum.

### *3.3.3 Depth estimation*

The blurring and deblurring measurements, $F_b$ and $F_d$, defined in Eqs. (12) and (17), respectively, can be substituted in the objective function in Eq. (7) to obtain

$$H(u) = \lambda \left\| g\left(\sigma(u_\infty)^2 - \sigma(u)^2\right) * f_0(u) - E\{f_0(x)\} \right\|^2 - K(x, u). \tag{18}$$

The blurring and deblurring approach can now be used to derive the solution for

$$\min_u H(u), \tag{19}$$

based on the constraint in Eq. (8). The complexity of the problem relies on how precise the depth is measured for each point. Although depth is an important cue, it seems that the relative depths, such as which object is in foreground and which is in background, are more important than the accurate depths. The blurring and deblurring approach is a point-wise optimization method. We used a method by deriving the best solution from the $d$ candidate depths in a sequence, $u_1, \cdots u_d$, to save the computational cost. To the optimization problem, the solution is to pick a candidate depth that has the minimization. The candidate depths were chosen so that $\sigma(u_i) - \sigma(u_{i-1}) = 0.2$ for $i = 2, \cdots, d$ in implementation. This procedure takes $\mathcal{O}(\gamma N^2 d)$, where $\gamma N^2$ is the ratio of edged and textured pixels in an image of $N^2$ pixels, point-wise blurring and deblurring operations to determine the depth map of the image.

## 4. Depth refinement and image deblurring

The blurring and deblurring measurements are only able to determine the depths of edge and texture points. However, if blurring and deblurring with Gaussian kernel of any variance are applied to a sufficiently large patch of constant value, it will yield a patch of constant value. Therefore, the proposed approach cannot reliably determine the depths of points in smooth regions. Thus, we resort to another approach to derive the depths of smooth scene points.

On the other hand, all in focus is to generate an image that is focused everywhere or to transfer the depth map of an image to a depth map in focal plane. Therefore, an all-in-focus image can be generated by the deblurring process. Practically, since a deblurring process is very sensitive to overestimated depth, if there are overestimated depths in images, the deblurring process can hamper the all-in-focus result and render a visually unacceptable image.

This problem cannot be trivially solved by subtracting a depth from all the points because the value to subtract is not easy to determine. This value should be large enough to stabilize the deblurring process and at the same time small enough so that the depths are not underestimated too much, rendering a blurred all-in-focus image. We used two methods, viz., depth quantization and TV deblurring process, to rectify the effects caused from the depth estimation error.

### 4.1 Depths of smooth scene points

We followed [6] to estimate the depth at edges and texture followed by propagation of the results to other points. In our method, we use Canny edge detector [10] to decide whether a point is an edged or textured point. The depths of these points (called Canny points) were then estimated from the blurring and deblurring approach. For convenience, we called the remaining points as the smooth points.

The propagation algorithm to derive the depths of smooth points was based on the solution of the Dirichlet problem [11], which addresses the temperature distribution from the boundary to the interior of a medium. The solution of the Dirichlet problem is based on two principles: the maximum principle and the uniqueness principle. The maximum principle states that the interior temperature lies between the maximum boundary temperature and the minimum boundary temperature, and the uniqueness principle states that the solution of the problem is unique. In our approach, we regarded the temperature as the depth and defined the boundary points as the union of the smooth points at the border and the non-smooth points of an image. The depth was first assigned to the smooth points at the border of the image. Then, we used the solution of the Dirichlet problem to derive the depth of the smooth points inside the image. By this approach, the depths of the smooth points were never larger than those of the enclosing points.

The steps of the depth propagation procedure are as follows. First, we normalized the depths of the Canny points by setting the depth of the point farthest from the camera as 1. Then, we assigned depths to the smooth points on the borders of the image. Because the top border of an image is usually the background, the depth of the smooth points on that border was assigned the value 1. For a smooth point on the left-hand, right-hand, and bottom borders, we assigned the depth of the closest non-smooth point. **Figure 5** demonstrates an example how the depths are propagated to an image.

### 4.2 Depth quantization

For the quantization process, a depth can be approximated by a layer. The motivation of the idea was from the scalar quantization in compression. Via the quantization process, a coefficient can be approximated. In the process, the layer $L$ is a parameter. From the results in Section 3.3.3, the histogram of the depths was calculated firstly. The representative (anchor) depth, $a_1$, for layer 1 was always assigned as the minimum depth of all the depths. When the depths are partitioned into two layers, we proposed the following optimization to determine the anchor depth of layer 2, $a_2$:

$$\min_{a_2} \sum_{z_i \in \, layer\ 1} (z_i - a_1)^2 + \sum_{z_i \in \, layer\ 2} (z_i - a_2)^2, \tag{20}$$

where $a_2$ is subject to $a_2 > z_i > a_1$, for each $z_i$ in layer 1, and $z_i \geq a_2$, for each $z_i$ in layer 2. By recursively subdividing a depth layer to acquire two more depth layers, the procedure can be applied to acquire $L$ layers. The depths in the layer are updated to be the depth of the anchor if the anchor depth of a layer is determined. For instance, the depth $z_i$ in layer $j$ is assigned as $a_j$. Hence, $z_i - a_j$ for $z_i$ in layer $j$ is the error in approximating $z_i$ with $a_j$. In the approximation, the anchor depth can be found from Eq. (20), which has the minimization of the error.

By sampling a few depths as candidate anchor depths firstly, the anchor depth $a_2$ in Eq. (20) can be derived. Next, we set each candidate as $a_2$ to calculate the average error from Eq. (20). With the help of the histogram of the depths, this process can

| | | | | | | | | | |
|---|---|---|---|---|---|---|---|---|---|
| | | | | | | | | | |
| 0.9 | | | 0.8 | 1 | | | 0.9 | | |
| | 0.9 | 0.8 | | 0.9 | 0.8 | | | 0.8 | 0.9 |
| 0.8 | | | | | | 0.7 | | 0.8 | 0.8 |
| | | | | | | 0.6 | 0.5 | 0.5 | 0.6 |
| 0.6 | 0.5 | | | | | | 0.4 | | |
| | 0.4 | | | | | | 0.3 | | 0.3 |
| 0.3 | | 0.2 | | 0.1 | 0.1 | | | 0.2 | |

| | | | | | | | | | |
|---|---|---|---|---|---|---|---|---|---|
| 1 | 1 | 1 | 1 | 1 | 1 | 1 | 1 | 1 | 1 |
| 0.9 | | | 0.8 | 1 | | | 0.9 | | 1 |
| 0.9 | 0.9 | 0.8 | | 0.9 | 0.8 | | | 0.8 | 0.9 |
| 0.8 | | | | | | 0.7 | | 0.8 | 0.8 |
| 0.8 | | | | | | 0.6 | 0.5 | 0.5 | 0.6 |
| 0.6 | 0.5 | | | | | | 0.4 | | 0.6 |
| 0.6 | 0.4 | | | | | | 0.3 | | 0.3 |
| 0.3 | 0.3 | 0.2 | 0.2 | 0.1 | 0.1 | 0.1 | 0.1 | 0.2 | 0.3 |

| | | | | | | | | | |
|---|---|---|---|---|---|---|---|---|---|
| 1 | 1 | 1 | 1 | 1 | 1 | 1 | 1 | 1 | 1 |
| 0.9 | 0.9 | 0.9 | 0.8 | 1 | 0.9 | 0.9 | 0.9 | 0.9 | 1 |
| 0.9 | 0.9 | 0.8 | 0.8 | 0.9 | 0.8 | 0.8 | 0.8 | 0.8 | 0.9 |
| 0.8 | 0.8 | 0.7 | 0.7 | 0.7 | 0.7 | 0.7 | 0.7 | 0.8 | 0.8 |
| 0.8 | 0.7 | 0.6 | 0.6 | 0.6 | 0.6 | 0.6 | 0.5 | 0.5 | 0.6 |
| 0.6 | 0.5 | 0.5 | 0.5 | 0.4 | 0.4 | 0.4 | 0.4 | 0.4 | 0.6 |
| 0.6 | 0.4 | 0.4 | 0.3 | 0.3 | 0.3 | 0.3 | 0.3 | 0.3 | 0.3 |
| 0.3 | 0.3 | 0.2 | 0.2 | 0.1 | 0.1 | 0.1 | 0.1 | 0.2 | 0.3 |

**Figure 5.**
*An example of depth propagation to the interior smooth patches achieved by solving the Dirichlet problem. (top left) The depth map of non-smooth patches (the depth of patches farthest from the camera was set at 1), (top right) the depths assigned to the border patches, and (bottom) the depths of the interior smooth patches derived by solving the Dirichlet problem.*

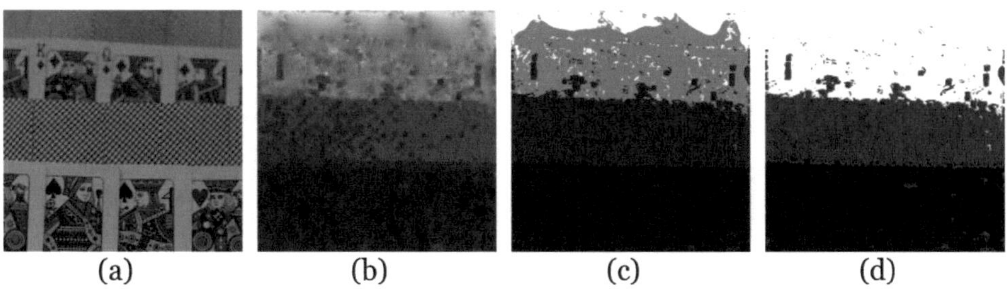

**Figure 6.**
*(a) The image composed of four depth layers. (b) Depth map derived by multi-scale blurring and deblurring approach. The top two layers of depths can hardly be distinguished. (c) The depth map is quantized to four layers. (d) The depth map is quantized to three layers.*

be efficiently achieved. So, the anchor depth is the depth in the candidate depths that yields the smallest average error. **Figure 6** shows the estimated depth map and the depth quantization results on an image, composed of four layers of depths. After quantization, some outliers in **Figure 6(b)** are removed.

### 4.3 Deblurring process

Patch $y$ can be modeled as $g(\sigma) * x$ where $x$ and $y$ are vectors, $x$ is the vector of the scene patch $X$ ($x = vec(X)$), and $\sigma$ is the out-of-focus blurriness of $x$ in $y$. The deblurring process restores $x$ by

$$\min_x \frac{\mu}{2} \|y - g(\sigma) * x\|^2 + \|D_1 X\|_1 + \|D_2 X\|_1, \tag{21}$$

where $\mu$ is a Lagrangian multiplier and $\|D_1X\|_1$ and $\|D_2X\|_1$ denote the discrete total variation of $X$ in horizontal and vertical directions, respectively. The $g(\sigma) * x$ can be represented as a matrix–vector multiplication. Eq. (21) can be solved by an efficient variable splitting technique, as described in Ref. [12].

## 5. Experimental results

We will demonstrate the depth estimation results and some applications related to the estimated depth map including all in focus, refocusing, defocus magnification, and 2D to 3D conversion. We use synthetic images, real images, and video frames to show the performance of the method.

### 5.1 Synthetic image

First, we evaluated the depth estimations on synthetic images. The scene images with the ground truth depth map are from [13], but the images and depth maps are not aligned. The proposed method is allowed to estimate the blurriness from a blur image; however, the given scene image is near to an all-in-focus image. Therefore, we align the depth map and the original image by nearest neighbor scaling method and then apply Eq. (4) to generate a blur map according to the given depth map with some fixed camera parameters. The transformed Gaussian blur kernels are controlled in the range from 0 to 8. A blur image is synthesized when the original scene image is convolved with the corresponding blur map. Two sets of the original scene images, depth maps of the ground truth, synthetic blurred images, and estimated depth maps are shown in **Figure** 7 (a), (b), (c), and (d), respectively. Perceptually, the estimated depth maps correspond to the ground truth depth maps with outlines.

(a) (b) (c) (d)

**Figure 7.**
*Datasets for the blurriness estimation. (a) Original scene image. (b) The ground truth depth map. (c) Synthetic blurred input images. (d) Estimated depth map.*

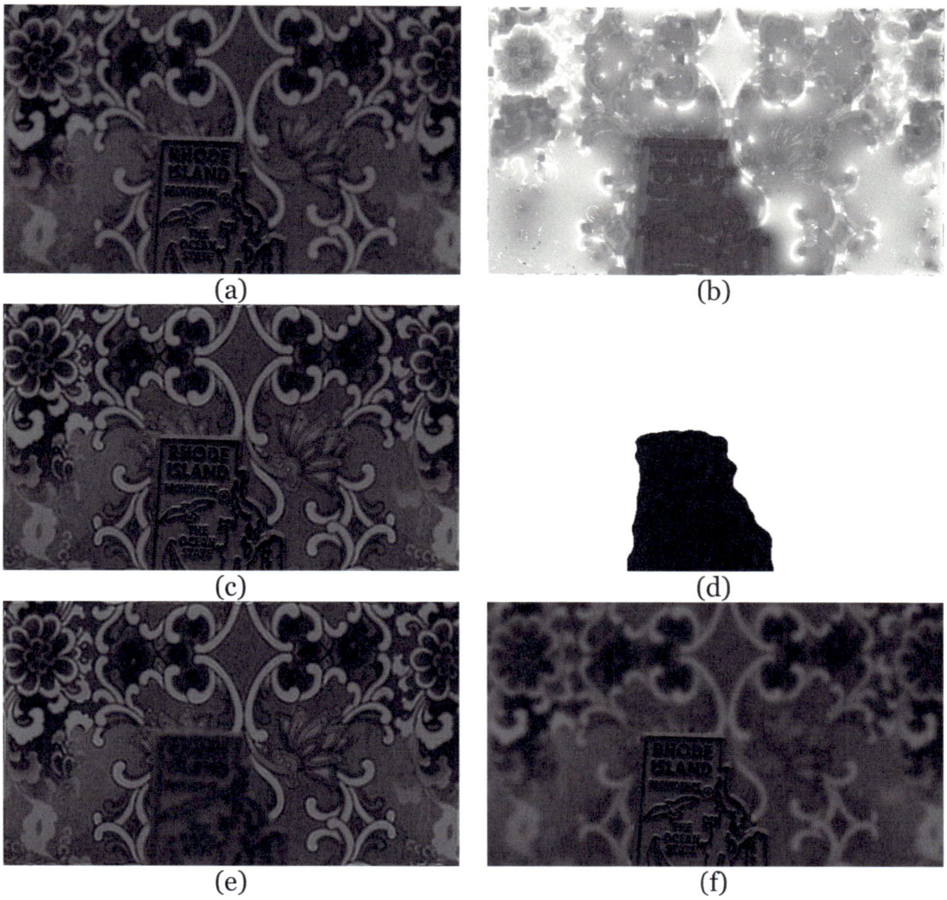


**Figure 8.**
*(a) The original image. (b) Estimated depth map. (c) All-in-focus image, derived with the depth map in (a). (d) Quantized depth map into two layers. The darker area is the foreground, and the bright area is the background. (e) Refocus image. (f) Defocus magnification image.*

## 5.2 Real image

Second, we set real images to the depth estimation method. **Figure 8** shows the results on a two-layer image, and the input image (a) is from [14]. The estimated depth map, synthesized all-in-focus image, quantized depth map, refocus image,

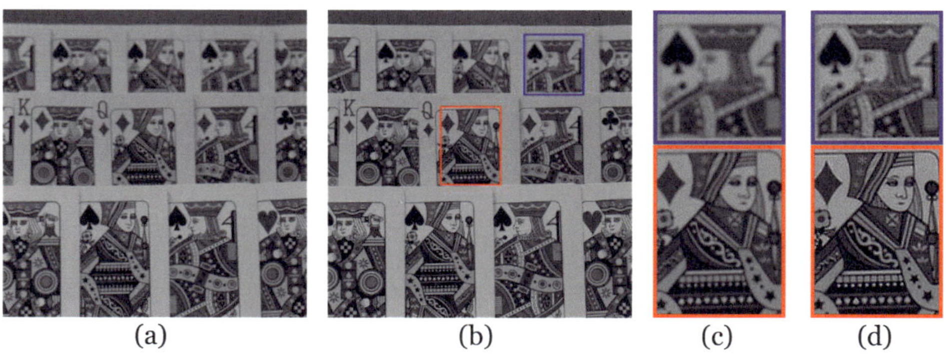


**Figure 9.**
*(a) The poker card image. (b) Synthetic all-in-focus image from the estimated depth map. (c) Magnified regions from (a). (d) Magnified regions from (b).*

and defocus magnification image are shown in **Figure 8(b)–(f)**, respectively. With the quantized depth map, the applications of refocusing and defocus magnification can be manipulated from the all-in-focus image. Therefore, if obtaining a high quality of the depth map and all-in-focus image, the performance of these applications will be great.

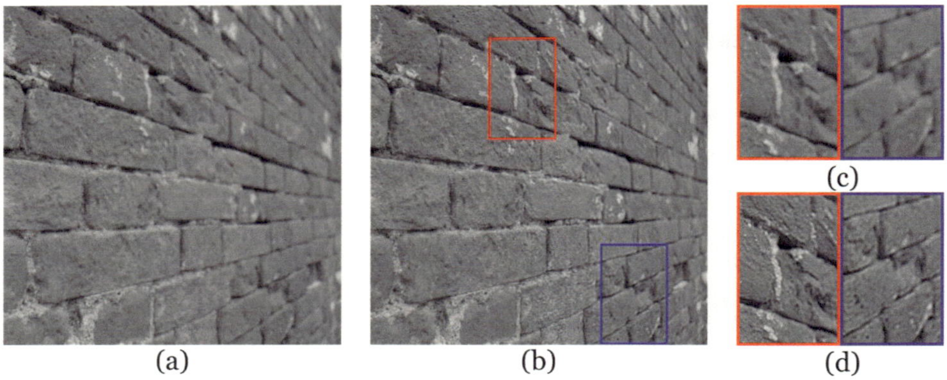


**Figure 10.**
*(a) The slanting brick wall image. (b) Synthetic all-in-focus image from the estimated depth map. (c) Magnified regions from (a). (d) Magnified regions from (b).*

**Figure 11.**
*2D to 3D conversion. (a) Input image (left-eye image). (b) Synthesized right-eye image. (c) Synthesized anaglyph 3D image.*

**Figures 9** and **10** present the performance of the all-in-focus image. **Figure 9(a)** is a three-layer poker card image, and the camera was focused on the third row of cards. The blurriness increased from the bottom part of the image to the top. So, the first and second rows of cards are out of focus. **Figure 9(b)** shows the synthesized all-in-focus image, and (c) and (d) show the corresponding magnified regions from (a) and (b), respectively. **Figure 10(a)** was captured from a ramp of brick wall. As the camera was focused on the leftmost part of the image, the blurriness of the brick wall progressively increased from the left part of the image to the right. **Figure 10(b)** shows the synthesized all-in-focus image, and (c) and (d) show the magnified regions. From these two sets of image, the results show a significant improvement when comparing to the original images.

### 5.3 Video frame

Third, we apply the method to the video frames. In this subsection, we show the performance of 2D to 3D conversion. The video frames in **Figure 11(a)** are used as the input left-eye images, which are from YouTube; (b) are the synthesized right-eye images, which are from left-eye images and corresponding depth maps; and (c) are the synthesized anaglyphs, which are from (a) and (b). With the anaglyph glasses, the 3D effect will be visualization. Combine the mobile device with the stereo image and VR device, such as Google Cardboard; the 3D effect also will be visualized.

## 6. Conclusions

In this chapter, a single-image depth estimation method was presented. The depth map was derived based on the characteristic curve of COC vs. depth of a camera. Applications to manipulate depth maps can be achieved by first deblurring an image to all in focus and then blurring the all-in-focus image. Thus, generation of an all-in-focus image from a depth map successfully is significant for the depth estimation method. Furthermore, the quality for 2D to 3D conversion also depends on the performance of depth estimation. The proposed depth estimation method makes it possible to produce high-quality all-in-focus images and 2D to 3D conversion, even from originals with a complex depth map layout.

## Author details

Shih-Shuo Tung and Wen-Liang Hwang*
Institute of Information Science, Academia Sinica, Taipei, Taiwan

*Address all correspondence to: whwang@iis.sinica.edu.tw

## References


[1] Grossmann P. Depth from focus. Pattern Recognition Letters. 1987;**5**(1): 63-69. DOI: 10.1016/0167-8655(87)90026-2

[2] Bulthoff HH, Mallot HA. Integration of depth modules: Stereo and shading. Journal of the Optical Society of America. A. 1998;**5**(10):1749-1758. DOI: 10.1364/JOSAA.5.001749

[3] Ullman S. The interpretation of structure from motion. Proceedings of the Royal Society of London B: Biological Sciences. 1979;**203**(1153): 405-426. DOI: 10.1098/rspb.1979.0006

[4] Levin A, Fergus R, Durand F, Freeman WT. Image and depth from a conventional camera with a coded aperture. ACM Transactions on Graphics. 2007;**26**(3). DOI: 10.1145/1276377.1276464

[5] Khoshelham K, Elberink SO. Accuracy and resolution of Kinect depth data for indoor mapping applications. Sensors. 2012;**12**(2):1437-1454. DOI: 10.3390/s120201437

[6] Bae S, Durand F. Defocus magnification. Computer Graphics Forum. 2007;**26**(3):571-579. DOI: 10.1111/j.1467-8659.2007.01080.x

[7] Zhuo S, Sim T. Defocus map estimation from a single image. Pattern Recognition. 2011;**44**(9):1852-1858. DOI: 10.1016/j.patcog.2011.03.009

[8] Tung SS, Shao HC, Hwang WL. Extending depth of field in noisy light field photography. In: Proceedings of the IEEE International Conference on Awareness Science and Technology (iCAST '17); 8-10 November 2017; Taiwan. pp. 127-131. DOI: 10.1109/ICAwST.2017.8256430

[9] Tung SS, Hwang WL. Multiple depth layers and all-in-focus image generations by blurring and deblurring operations. Pattern Recognition. 2017;**69**:184-198. DOI: 10.1016/j.patcog.2017.03.035

[10] Canny J. A computational approach to edge detection. IEEE Transactions on Pattern Analysis and Machine Intelligence. 1986;**8**(6):679-698. DOI: 10.1109/TPAMI.1986.4767851

[11] Doyle PG, Snell JL. Random Walks and Electric Networks. USA: The Mathematical Association of America; 1984. DOI: 10.5948/UPO9781614440222

[12] Wang Y, Yang J, Yin W, Zhang Y. A new alternating minimization algorithm for total variation image reconstruction. SIAM Journal on Imaging Sciences. 2008;**1**(3):248-272. DOI: 10.1137/080724265

[13] Saxena A, Chung SH, Ng AY. 3d depth reconstruction from a single still image. International Journal of Computer Vision. 2008;**76**(1):53-69. DOI: 10.1007/s11263-007-0071-y

[14] Zhang W, Cham WK. Single-image refocusing and defocusing. IEEE Transactions on Image Processing. 2012;**21**(2):873-882. DOI: 10.1109/TIP.2011.2162739

Chapter 4

# Recurrent Level Set Networks for Instance Segmentation

*Thi Hoang Ngan Le, Khoa Luu, Marios Savvides, Kha Gia Quach and Chi Nhan Duong*

## Abstract

Level set (LS)-based segmentation has been widely used in medical imaging domain. It however has some difficulty when dealing with multi-instance objects in the real world. Furthermore, LS's performance is generally quite sensitive to some initial settings and parameters such as the number of iterations. To address these issues and promote the classic LS methods to a new degree of performance in a trainable deep learning framework, we are presenting a novel approach contextual recurrent level sets (CRLS) for object instance segmentation. In the proposed networks, the curve deformation process is formed as a hidden state evolution procedure in gated recurrent units (GRUs) and updated by minimizing an energy functional composed of fitting forces and contour length.

**Keywords:** level sets, convolutional neural networks (CNNs), recurrent neural networks (RNNs), image segmentation, semantic segmentation

## 1. Introduction

One of the central goals of computer vision is object recognition and scene understanding. Humans are able to (1) possess a remarkable ability to parse an image simply by looking at them. (2) analyze an image and separate all the components present in it (3) recognize a new object that has never seen before based on observing a set of objects. The Holy Grail of a computer vision system is to able to perform as same tasks as humans are with the ability of across huge variations in pose, appearance, viewpoint, illumination, occlusion, etc. Obviously, this is a very difficult computational problem and involves in eventually making intelligent machines. An image understanding system can be roughly defined in four different subproblems, i.e., image classification, object detection, semantic segmentation, semantic instance segmentation, according to its level of complexity.

1. **Image classification:** assign a label to an image. In this subproblem, all the objects presenting in a scene are given one label, independent of its location.

2. **Object detection:** predict the bounding box around an object as well as the class of each object. This subproblem is also known as object localization.

3. **Semantic segmentation:** predict the semantic class of the individual pixels in an image. However this subproblem unable to distinguish different instances of the same class.

4. **Instance segmentation:** label as well as provide pixel-level segmentation to each object instance in the image. This subproblem is the higher level of semantic segmentation. It can be considered as a combination of the second subproblem and third problem.

This chapter focus on the problem of semantic instance segmentation by reformulating the classic LS contour evolution in a new learnable deep framework *recurrent level set* (*RLS*) that employs gated recurrent unit under the energy minimization of a LS functional. In the proposed RLS framework, the curve deformation process in the classic LS acts as a hidden state evolution procedure and updated by minimizing an energy functional composed of fitting forces and contour length. By sharing the convolutional features and collaborating with region proposal detection in a *fully end-to-end trainable framework*, we extend RLS to *Contextual RLS* (*CRLS*) to address semantic segmentation in the wild.

This book chapter is organized as follows: Section 2 introduce basic concept of both LS and deep learning including convolutional neural networks (CNNs) and recurrent neural networks (RNNs). The next two sections focus on contextual recurrent level set for object instance segmentation. The last section is targeting at experimental results which have been conducted on PASCAL VOC and COCO datasets.

## 2. Background

This section starts with introducing the convolutional neural networks (CNNs) models, and recurrent neural networks (RNNs), specialized artificial neural networks (ANNs) architecture particularly useful for computer vision problems. Then, we introduce active contour (AC) and a classic variational level set (LS) mechanism which have been used in image segmentation.

### 2.1 Convolutional neural networks

Convolutional neural networks (CNNs) [1–4] are a special case of fully connected multi-layer perceptrons that are mainly focusing on weight sharing to process grid-like topology data, i.e., an image. In CNNs, the spatial correlation of the signal is used to constrain the architecture in a more sensible way. There are two keys properties in their architecture, i.e., spatially shared weights and spatial pooling. These properties are made based on biological visual system which help them extremely useful for image applications. In such kind of network, the pooling layers aim at producing feature that are shift-invariant whereas the convolution layers is to lean visual representation. Since 2012, one of the most notable results in deep learning is the use of convolutional neural networks to obtain a remarkable improvement in object recognition for ImageNet classification challenge.

A typical convolutional network has multiple stages. Each stage contains one or many convolution layer, activation layer, pooling layer. The output of each stage is feature maps which are a set of 2D arrays. In its more general form, a convolutional network can be written as:

$$\begin{aligned}
\mathbf{h}^0 &= \mathbf{x} \\
\mathbf{h}^l &= pool^l\left(\sigma_l\left(\mathbf{w}^l\mathbf{h}^{l-1} + \mathbf{b}^l\right)\right), \forall l \in 1, 2, \ldots L \qquad (1) \\
\mathbf{o} = \mathbf{h}^L &= f(\mathbf{x}, \theta)
\end{aligned}$$

where $\mathbf{w}^l$, $\mathbf{b}^l$ are trainable parameters as in MLPs at layer $l$. $\mathbf{x} \in \mathrm{R}^{c \times h \times w}$ is vectorized from an input image with $c$ is color channels, $h$ is the image height and $w$ is the image width. $\mathbf{o} \in \mathrm{R}^{n \times h' \times w'}$ is vectorized from an array of dimension $h' \times w'$ of output vector (of dimension $n$). $pool^l$ is a (optional) pooling function at layer $l$.

The main difference between multi-layer neural networks (MLPs) and CNNs lies in the parameter matrices $\mathbf{w}_l$. In MLPs, the matrices can take any general form, while in CNNs these matrices are constraints to be Toeplitz matrices. That is, the columns are circularly shifted versions of the signal of various shifts for each columns in order to implement spatial correlation operation using matrix algebra. Furthermore, these matrices are very sparse because the image size is much bigger than the kernel size. Thus, the hidden unit $\mathbf{h}_l$ can be expressed as a discrete-time convolution between the kernel $\mathbf{w}_l$ and the previous hidden unit $\mathbf{h}_{l-1}$. A point-wise non-linearity and pooling are then applied on the hidden unit. There are numerous variants of CNNs architectures in the literature. However, their basic components are very similar which contains of convolutional layer, pooling layer, activation layer and fully connected layer.

- **Convolutional layer:** the convolutional layer aims to learn feature representations of the inputs and it is composed of several convolution kernels which are used to compute different feature maps. In a convolutional layer, each neuron of a feature map is connected to a region of neighboring neurons in the previous layer. The new feature map can be obtained by first convolving the input with a kernel and then applying an element-wise nonlinear activation function on the convolved results. The feature maps are obtained by using a set of different kernels.

- **Activation layer:** the activation function introduces nonlinearities to CNNs. This layer controls how the signal flows from one layer to the next, emulating how neurons are fired in our brain.

- **Pooling layer:** pooling layer is also called sampling layer to smooth the input from the convolutional layer. The pooling layer helps to (1) reduce the sensitivity of the filters to noise and variations. Pooling operation is usually placed between two convolutional layers. Each feature map of a pooling layer is connected to its corresponding feature map of the preceding convolutional layer.

- **Loss layer:** it is important to choose an appropriate loss function for a specific task. *Softmax* loss is a commonly used loss function which is essentially a combination of multinomial logistic loss and softmax. Softmax turns the predictions into non-negative values and normalizes them to get a probability distribution over classes. Such probabilistic predictions are used to compute the multinomial logistic loss.

- **Regularization:** regularization aims to reduce the overfitting problem during training. $l_p$-*norm*, Dropout, and DropConnect are some common regularization techniques have been developed to solve this.

- **Optimization:** data augmentation, weight initialization, stochastic gradient descent, batch normalization, shortcut connections are some common optimization techniques that will be discussed. Popular *data augmentation* methods are sampling, various photometric transformations, shifting, and greedy strategy. *Stochastic gradient descent* [5] (SGD) is the most popular technique used to update the parameter during backpropagation.

## 2.2 Recurrent neural networks

The Recurrent Neural Networks (RNNs) is an extremely powerful sequence model and was introduced in the early 1990s [6]. A typical RNNs contains three parts, namely sequential input data ($\mathbf{x}_t$), hidden state ($\mathbf{h}_t$) and sequential output data ($\mathbf{o}_t$).

RNNs contains a sequence of elements and each element performs the similar task. The input of future element depends on the output of current element. The RNNs contains one or many input and one or many output depending on the applications. Some examples, of RNNs architecture are given in **Figure 1**.

In RNNs, the activation of the hidden states at timestep $t$ is computed as a function $\mathbf{F}$ of the current input symbol $\mathbf{x}_t$ and the previous hidden states $\mathbf{h}_{t-1}$. The output at time $t$ is calculated as a function $\mathbf{G}$ of the current hidden state $\mathbf{h}_t$ as follows:

$$\begin{aligned} \mathbf{h}_t &= \mathbf{F}(\mathbf{U}\mathbf{x}_t + \mathbf{W}\mathbf{h}_{t-1}) \\ \mathbf{o}_t &= \mathbf{F}(\mathbf{V}\mathbf{h}_t) \end{aligned} \tag{2}$$

where $\mathbf{W}$ is the state-to-state recurrent weight matrix, $\mathbf{U}$ is the input-to-hidden weight matrix, $\mathbf{V}$ is the hidden-to-output weight matrix. $\mathbf{F}$ is usually a logistic sigmoid function or a hyperbolic tangent function and $\mathbf{G}$ is defined as a softmax function.

Most work on RNNs has made use of the method of backpropagation through time (BPTT) [7] to train the parameter set $(\mathbf{U}, \mathbf{V}, \mathbf{W})$ and propagate error backward through time. In classic backpropagation, the error or loss function is defined as:

$$E(\mathbf{o}, \mathbf{y}) = \sum_t \left\| \mathbf{o}_t - \mathbf{y}_t \right\|^2 \tag{3}$$

where $\mathbf{o}_t$ is prediction and $y_t$ is labeled groundtruth.

For a specific weight $\mathbf{W}$, the update rule for gradient descent is defined as $\mathbf{W}^{new} = \mathbf{W} - \gamma \frac{\partial E}{\partial \mathbf{W}}$, where $\gamma$ is the learning rate. In RNNs model, the gradients of the error with respect to our parameters $\mathbf{U}$, $\mathbf{V}$ and $\mathbf{W}$ are learned using stochastic gradient descent (SGD) and chain rule of differentiation.

There are two popular improvements of RNNs in order to solve the problems of exploding and vanishing when dealing with long time dependency.

- **Long short time memory:** to address the issue of learning long-term dependencies, Hochreiter and Schmidhuber [8] proposed Long Short-Term Memory (LSTM), which is able to maintain a separate memory cell inside it that updates and exposes its content only when deemed necessary. Similar to RNNs, LSTMs are defined under a chain like structure, but the repeating module has a different structure. Instead of having a single neural network

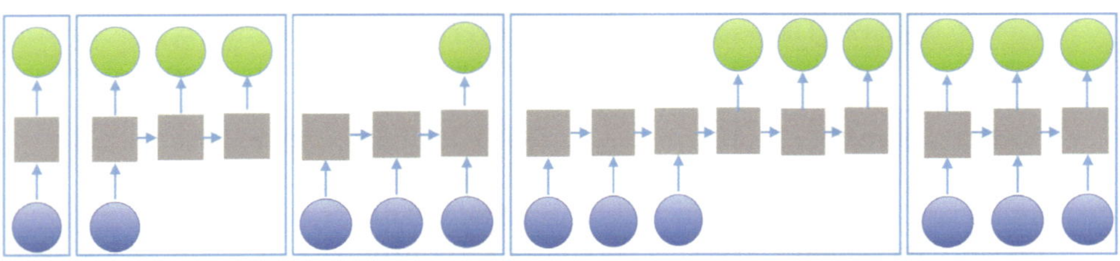

**Figure 1.**
*Example of RNNs architecture.*

layer (single tanh layer), LSTMS have four neural networks in each layer and they are interacting in a very special way. The key to LSTMs is the cell state ($C_t$) which has the ability to remove or add information by optionally letting information through. Gates are composed out of a sigmoid layer and a pointwise multiplication operation.

- **Gated recurrent units:** to make each recurrent unit adaptively capture dependencies of different time scales, [9] proposed gated recurrent unit (GRU) as an extension of RNN. Similar LSTM unit, GRU contains gating units that control the flow of information inside the unit. However, GRU does not have separate memory cells. By using leaky integration, GRU is able to fully expose its memory content each timestep and balance between the previous memory content and the new memory content strictly. Notably, its adaptive time constant is controlled by the update gate. In traditional RNNs, the content of activation unit is always replaces by a new value calculated from the current input and the previous hidden state. Instead of replacing, GRU jsut adds the new content on top and still keeps the existing content. This addition provides shortcut paths that bypass multiple temporal steps. In GRUs, thank to these shortcuts, the error is back-propagated easily without too quickly vanishing as a result of passing through multiple, bounded nonlinearities. Thus it help to reduce the difficulty due to vanishing gradients. Furthermore, using the addition, each unit is able to remember the existence of a specific feature in the input stream for a long series of steps.

### 2.3 Variational level set

Variational level set is an implicit implementation of active contour (AC). The main ideas of applying AC for image segmentation is to start with an initial random (guess) contour $C$ which is represented in a form of closed curves. The curve is then iteratively adjusted by shrinking or expanding under an image-driven forces until it reach to the boundaries of the desired objects. The entire process is called contour evolution or curve evolution, denoted as $\frac{\partial C}{\partial t}$.

There are two main approaches in active contours: snakes and level sets. Snakes explicitly move predefined snake points based on an energy minimization scheme, while level set approaches move contours implicitly as a particular level of a function.

Level set (LS)-based or implicit active contour models have provided more flexibility and convenience for the implementation of active contours, thus, they have been used in a variety of image processing and computer vision tasks. The basic idea of the implicit active contour is to represent the initial curve $C$ implicitly within a higher dimensional function, called the level set function $\phi(x,y) : \Omega \rightarrow R$, such as: $C = (x,y) : \phi(x,y) = 0, \forall(x,y) \in \Omega$, where $\Omega$ denotes the entire image plane.

A zero level set function is used to formulate the contour, i.e., the contour evolution is equivalent to the evolution of the level set function, i.e., $\frac{\partial C}{\partial t} = \frac{\partial \phi(x,y)}{\partial t}$. The reason of using the zero level set is that a contour can be defined as the border between a positive area and a negative area. Thus, everything on the zero area belongs to the contour and it is identified by signed distance function as follows:

$$\phi(x) = \begin{cases} d(x,C)) & \text{if } x \text{ is inside } C \\ 0 & \text{if } x \text{ is on } C \\ -d(x,C)) & \text{if } x \text{ is outside } C \end{cases} \tag{4}$$

where $d(x,C)$ denotes the distance from an arbitrary position to the curve.

The computation is performed on the same dimension as the image plane $\Omega$, therefore, the computational cost of level set methods is high and the convergence speed is quite slow.

Under the scenarios of image segmentation, we consider an image in 2D space, $\Omega$. The level set is to find the boundary $C$ of an open set $\omega \in \Omega$, which is defined as: $C = \partial\omega$. In LS framework, the boundary $C$ can be represented by the zero level set $\phi$ as follows:

$$\forall(x,y) \in \Omega \begin{cases} C = & \{(x,y) : \phi(x,y) = 0\} \\ inside(C)) & \{(x,y) : \phi(x,y) > 0\} \\ output(C)) & \{(x,y) : \phi(x,y) < 0\} \end{cases} \tag{5}$$

Under the image segmentation problem, entire domain of an image **I** is presented by $\Omega$ which contains three regions corresponding to: inside contour (¿0), on contour (=0) and outside the contour (¡0). Clearly, the zero LS function $\phi$ partitions the region $\Omega$ into two regions: region inside $\omega$ (foreground), denoted as inside (C) and region outside $\omega$ (background) denoted as outside (C). Using the zero level set function, the length of the contour C and the area inside the contour C are defined as follows:

$$\begin{aligned} Length(C) &= \int_\Omega |\nabla H(\phi(x,y))| dxdy = \int_\Omega \delta(\phi(x,y)) |\nabla \phi(x,y)| dxdy \\ Area(C) &= \int_\Omega H(\phi(x,y)) dxdy \end{aligned} \tag{6}$$

where $H_\varepsilon(\cdot)$ is a Heaviside function.

Typically, the LS-based segmentation methods start with an initial level set $\phi_0$ and an given image **I**. The LS updating process is performed via gradient descent by minimizing an energy function which defined based on the difference of image features, such as color and texture, between foreground and background. The fitting term in LS model is defined by the inside contour energy ($E_1$) and outside contour energy ($E_2$).

$$E = E_1 + E_2 = \int_{insideC} \left(I_{(x,y)} - c_1\right)^2 dxdy + \int_{outsideC} \left(I_{(x,y)} - c_2\right)^2 dxdy \tag{7}$$

where $c_1$ and $c_2$ are the average intensity inside and outside the contour $C$, respectively.

One of the most popular region based active contour models is proposed by Chan-Vese (CV) [10]. In this model the boundaries are not defined by gradients and the curve evolution is based on the general Mumford-Shah (MS) [11] formulation of image segmentation as shown in Eq. (8).

$$E = \int_\Omega |\mathbf{I} - u|^2 dxdy + \int_{\Omega/C} |\nabla u|^2 dxdy + \nu Length(C) \tag{8}$$

CV's model is an alternative form of MS's model which restricts the solution to piecewise constant intensities and it has successfully segmented an image into two regions, each having a distinct mean of pixel intensity by minimizing the following energy functional.

$$E(c_1, c_2, \phi) = \mu \text{Area}(\omega_1) + \nu \text{Length}(C) + \lambda_1 \int_{\omega_1} |\mathbf{I}(x,y) - c_1|^2 dxdy + \lambda_2 \int_{\omega_2} |\mathbf{I}(x,y) - c_2|^2 dxdy \tag{9}$$

where $c_1$ and $c_2$ are two constants. The parameters $\mu, \nu, \lambda_1, \lambda_2$ are positive parameters and usually fixing $\lambda_1 = \lambda_2 = 1$ and $\mu = 0$. Thus, we can ignore the first term in Eq. (9). Thus the energy functional is rewritten as follows:

$$\begin{aligned} E(c_1, c_2, \phi) = \mu \int_\Omega H(\phi(x,y))dxdy + \nu \int_\Omega \delta(\phi(x,y))|\nabla\phi(x,y)|dxdy \\ + \lambda_1 \int_{\omega_1} |\mathbf{I}(x,y) - c_1|^2 dxdy + \lambda_2 \int_{\omega_2} |\mathbf{I}(x,y) - c_2|^2 dxdy \end{aligned} \tag{10}$$

For numerical approximations, the $\delta$ function needs a regularizing term for smoothing. In most cases, the Heaviside function $H$ and Dirac delta function $\delta$ are defined as in Eq. (11) and Eq. (12), respectively.

$$H_\varepsilon(x) = \frac{1}{2}\left(1 + \frac{2}{\pi}\arctan\left(\frac{x}{\varepsilon}\right)\right) \text{and } \delta_\varepsilon(x) = H'(x) = \frac{1}{\pi}\frac{\varepsilon}{\varepsilon^2 + x^2} \tag{11}$$

$$\delta_\varepsilon(x) = H'(x) = \frac{1}{\pi}\frac{\varepsilon}{\varepsilon^2 + x^2} \tag{12}$$

As $\varepsilon \to 0$, $\delta_\varepsilon \to \delta$, and $H_\varepsilon \to H$. Using Heaviside function $H$, the Eq. 10 becomes Eq. 13.

$$\begin{aligned} E(c_1, c_2, \phi) = \mu \int_\Omega H(\phi(x,y))dxdy + \nu \int_\Omega \delta(\phi(x,y))|\nabla\phi(x,y)|dxdy \\ + \lambda_1 \int_\Omega |\mathbf{I}(x,y) - c_1|^2 H(\phi(x,y))dxdy + \lambda_2 \int_\Omega |\mathbf{I}(x,y) - c_2|^2 (1 - H(\phi(x,y)))dxdy \end{aligned} \tag{13}$$

In the implementation, they choose $\varepsilon = 1$. For fixed $c_1$ and $c_2$, gradient descent equation with respect to $\phi$ is:

$$\frac{\partial\phi(x,y)}{\partial t} = \delta_\varepsilon\, \phi(x,y)\left[\nu\kappa\, \phi(x,y) - \mu - \lambda_1(\mathbf{I}(x,y) - c_1)^2 + \lambda_2(\mathbf{I}(x,y) - c_2)^2\right] \tag{14}$$

where $\delta_\varepsilon$ is a regularized form of Dirac delta function and $c_1$, $c_2$ are the mean of inside the contour $\omega_{in}$ and the mean of the outside of the contour $\omega_{out}$, respectively. The curvature $\kappa$ is given by:

$$\kappa(\phi(x,y)) = -\text{div}\left(\frac{\Delta\phi}{|\Delta\phi|}\right) = -\frac{\phi_{xx}\phi_y^2 - 2\phi_x\phi_y\phi_{xy} + \phi_{yy}\phi_x^2}{\left(\phi_x^2 + \phi_y^2\right)^{1.5}} \tag{15}$$

where $\partial_x\varphi_t$, $\partial_y\varphi_t$ and $\partial_{xx}\varphi_t$, $\partial_{yy}\varphi_t$ are the first and second derivatives of $\varphi_t$ with respect to $x$ and $y$ directions. For fixed $\phi$, gradient descent equation with respect to $c_1$ and $c_2$ are:

$$c_1 = \frac{\sum_{x,y}\mathbf{I}(x,y)H(\phi(x,y))}{\sum_{x,y}H(\phi(x,y))} \text{and } c_2 = \frac{\sum_{x,y}\mathbf{I}(x,y)(1 - H(\phi(x,y)))}{\sum_{x,y}(1 - H(\phi(x,y)))} \tag{16}$$

herein, we use notation $\varphi_t$ to indicate $\varphi$ at the iteration $t^{th}$ in order to distinguish the $\varphi$ at different iterations. Under this formulation, the curve evolution is shown as a time series process which helps to give better visualization of reformulating LS. From this point, we redefine the curve updating in a time series form for the LS function $\varphi_t$ as in Eq. (17).

$$\varphi_{t+1} = \varphi_t + \eta \frac{\partial \varphi_t}{\partial t} \tag{17}$$

The LS at time $t+1$ depends on the previous LS at time $t$ and the curve evolution $\frac{\partial \varphi_t}{\partial t}$ with a learning rate $\eta$.

## 3. Recurrent level set for object instance segmentation

To reformulate level set under a RNNs/GRUs deep framework, we need to solve the following problems:

- **Input:** How to generate a sequential data $x_t$ from a single image $I$ if we treat $\phi_t$ in LS as hidden state $h_t$ in RNNs with the same updating manner?

- **Output:** In the segmentation problem by LS, the binary mask corresponding to foreground and background is computed by one forward process with many iterations whereas the RNNs is computed by forward procedure and learnt by backward procedure. How to compute the error and perform backward procedure in LS framework?

- **Update rule:** Does the update rule in LS work in the same fashion as the forward procedure in RNNs/GRUs deep framework?

As shown in **Table** 1, one of the most challenging problems of reformulating LS as RNNs is data configuration. RNNs work on sequential data whereas LS uses single image as input and produce a mask as single image too. The first question here is *how to generate sequential data from a single image*. Moreover, there are two source inputs used in LS, i.e., an input image $I$ and an initial contour which is treated as initial LS function $\phi_0$ and updated by Eq. (17). That means we need to generate a sequential data $x_t$ $(t = 1, \cdots, N)$ from single image $\mathbf{I}$ in our proposed RLS. In order to achieve this goal, we define a function $g(\mathrm{I}, \phi_{t-1})$ as in Eq. (18).

$$\mathbf{x}_t = g(\mathbf{I}, \phi_{t-1}) = \phi_{t-1} + \eta\left[\kappa(\phi_{t-1}) - \mathbf{U}_g(\mathbf{I} - c_1)^2 + \mathbf{W}_g(\mathbf{I} - c_2)^2\right] \tag{18}$$

In Eq. (18), $c_1$ and $c_2$ are average values of inside and outside of the contour presented by the LS function $\phi_{t-1}$ and defined in Eq. (16). $\kappa$ denotes the curvature and defined in Eq. (15). $\mathbf{U}_g$ and $\mathbf{W}_g$ are two matrices that control the force inside and outside of the contour.

In such equation, the curve evolution in the proposed RLS functions as same as in the traditional LS defined by Eq. (14), i.e. the input at iteration $t^{th}$, $\mathbf{x}_t$, is updated based on the input image $\mathbf{I}$ and the previous LS function $\phi_{t-1}$. In our proposed RLS, $\mathbf{x}_t$ is considered to be sequential input whereas LS updating $\phi_t$ is treated as hidden state updating. Notably, the initial contour in LS function plays the role as initial hidden state as randomly generated. The relationship among $\mathbf{I}$, $\mathbf{x}_t$, and $\phi_t$ are given in **Figure** 2.

So far, the question of generating input sequence from the single image $\mathbf{I}$ has been answered. In the proposed RLS, we use the same input as defined in LS problem, namely the input image $\mathbf{I}$ and the initial $\phi_0$. We generate sequential data $\mathbf{x}_t$ from the input as single image. The next challenging problem is how to generate the hidden state $\phi_t$ from the input data $x_t$ and the previous hidden state $\phi_{t-1}$. Under the same intuition of proposing GRUs [9], the procedure of generating hidden state $\phi_t$

| | Input | Update | Output |
|---|---|---|---|
| CLS | Image $\mathbf{I}$<br>Initial LS function $\phi_0$ | $\phi_{t+1} = \phi_t + \eta \frac{\partial \phi_t}{\partial t}$<br>$\frac{\partial \phi_t}{\partial t} = \delta_\varepsilon(\phi_t[\nu\kappa(\phi_t - \mu\,\lambda_1(\mathbf{I}-c_1)^2 + \lambda_2(\mathbf{I}-c_2)^2])$ | $\phi_N$ |
| GRUs | Sequence $x_1, x_2, ..x_N$<br>Initial hidden state $h_0$ | $\mathbf{z}_t = f(\mathbf{U}_z\mathbf{x}_t + \mathbf{W}_z\mathbf{h}_{t-1})$<br>$\mathbf{r}_t = f(\mathbf{U}_r\mathbf{x}_t + \mathbf{W}_r\mathbf{h}_{t-1})$<br>$\tilde{\mathbf{h}}_t = h(\mathbf{U}_h\mathbf{x}_t + \mathbf{W}_h(\mathbf{h}_{t-1} \circ \mathbf{r}_t))$<br>$\mathbf{h}_t = (1-\mathbf{z}_t)\mathbf{h}_{t-1} + \mathbf{z}_t\tilde{\mathbf{h}}_t$<br>$h$: Tanh<br>$f$: Sigmoid or Tanh | $\mathcal{G}(\mathbf{V}\mathbf{h}_N)$<br>$\mathcal{G}$: softmax |
| RLS | Image $\mathbf{I}$<br>Initial LS function $\phi_0$ | $\mathbf{x}_t = \kappa\left(\phi_{t-1} - \mathbf{U}_g(\mathbf{I}-c_1)^2 + \mathbf{W}_g(\mathbf{I}-c_2)^2\right)$<br>$\mathbf{z}_t = \sigma(\mathbf{U}_z\mathbf{x}_t + \mathbf{W}_z\phi_{t-1} + \mathbf{b}_z)$<br>$\mathbf{r}_t = \sigma(\mathbf{U}_r\mathbf{x}_t + \mathbf{W}_r\phi_{t-1} + \mathbf{b}_r)$<br>$\tilde{\mathbf{h}}_t = h(\mathbf{U}_y\mathbf{x}_t + \mathbf{W}_y(\phi_{t-1} \circ \mathbf{r}_t) + \mathbf{b}_y)$<br>$\phi_t = (1-\mathbf{z}_t)\phi_{t-1} + \mathbf{z}_t\mathbf{h}t$<br>$h$: Tanh<br>$\sigma$: Sigmoid | $\mathcal{G}(\mathbf{V}\phi_N + b_V)$<br>$\mathcal{G}$: softmax |

**Table 1.**
*Comparison of input, update rule and output used in traditional LS, GRUs, and our proposed RLS.*

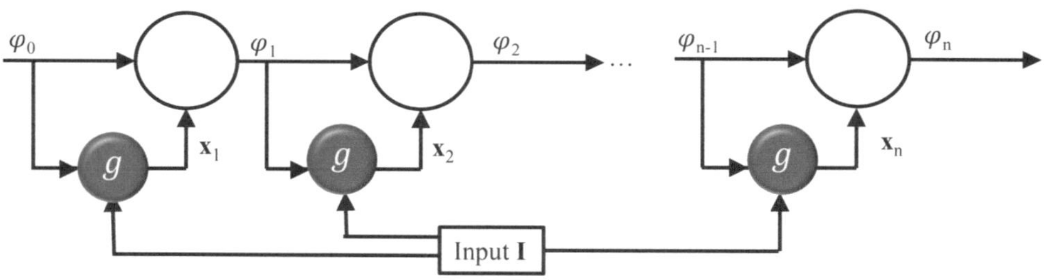


**Figure 2.**
*The visualization of generating sequence input data $\mathbf{x}_t$ and hidden state $\phi_t$ from the input image $\mathbf{I}$ and the initial LS function $\phi_0$.*

is based on the updated gate $\mathbf{z}_t$, the candidate memory content $\tilde{\mathbf{h}}_t$ and the previous activation unit $\phi_{t-1}$ as the rule given in Eq. (19).

$$\phi_t = \mathbf{z}_t\tilde{\mathbf{h}}_t + (1-\mathbf{z}_t)\phi_{t-1} \tag{19}$$

The update gate $\mathbf{z}_t$, which controls how much of the previous memory content is to be forgotten and how much of the new memory content is to be added is defined as in Eq. (20).

$$\mathbf{z}_t = \sigma(\mathbf{U}_z\mathbf{x}_t + \mathbf{W}_z\phi_{t-1} + \mathbf{b}_z) \tag{20}$$

where $\sigma$ is a sigmoid function and $\mathbf{b}_z$ is the update bias. However, the propose RLS does not have any mechanism to control the degree to which its state is exposed, but exposes the whole state each time in such naive definition. To address that issue, the new candidate memory content $y_t$ is computed. as in Eq. (21).

$$\tilde{\mathbf{h}}_t = tanh\left(\mathbf{U}_{\tilde{h}}\mathbf{x}_t + \mathbf{W}_{\tilde{h}}(\phi_{t-1} \odot \mathbf{r}_t) + \mathbf{b}_{\tilde{h}}\right) \tag{21}$$

where $\odot$ denotes an element-wise multiplication, $\mathbf{b}_{\tilde{h}}$ is the hidden bias. The reset gate $\mathbf{r}_t$ is computed similarly to the update gate as in Eq. (22).

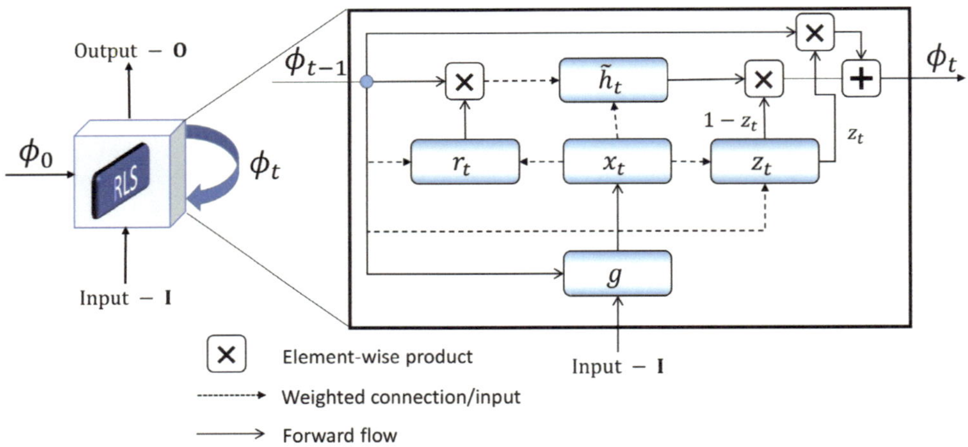


**Figure 3.**
*The proposed RLS network for curve updating process under the sequential evolution and its forward computation of curve evolution from time t − 1 to time t.*

$$\mathbf{r}_t = \sigma(\mathbf{U}_r\mathbf{x}_t + \mathbf{W}_r\phi_{t-1} + \mathbf{b}_r) \tag{22}$$

where $\mathbf{b}_r$ is the reset bias. When $\mathbf{r}_t$ is close to 0 (off), the reset gate effectively makes the unit act as if it is reading the first symbol of an input sequence, allowing it to forget the previously computed state. The output $\mathbf{o}$ is computed from the current hidden states $\phi_t$ and then a softmax function is applied to obtain foreground/background segmentation $\hat{\mathbf{y}}$ given the input image as follows:

$$\begin{aligned} \hat{\mathbf{y}} &= \text{softmax}(\mathbf{o}) \\ \mathbf{o} &= \mathbf{V}\phi_t + \mathbf{b}_V \end{aligned} \tag{23}$$

where $\mathbf{V}$ is weighted matrix between hidden state and output. **Figure 4** (left) illustrate the proposed RLS in folded mode where the input of the network is defined as the same as the LS model, i.e., a given input image $\mathbf{I}$ and an initial LS function $\phi_0$. In our proposed RLS, the curve evolution from $\phi_t$ at present time step $t$ to the future $\phi_{t+1}$ at time $t+1$ is designed in the same fashion as the hidden state in GRUs and is illustrated in **Figure 4** (right) where $\phi_{t+1}$ depends on both previous LS function $\phi_t$ and the present input $\mathbf{x}_{t+1}$. We have summarized the comparison among LS, GRUs and our proposed RLS in **Table 1** and visulized the relationship between LS and GRUs as **Figure 3**. It is easy to see that RLS uses the same input as in traditional LS where the curve evolution (i.e., update procedure) and output in the proposed RLS follows similar fashion as in GRUs.

We summarize the proposed building block RLS in Algorithm 1.

---

**Algorithm 1.** Algorithm of the proposed building block RLS

---

**Input:** Given an image $\mathbf{I}$, an initial level set function $\phi_0$, time step $N$, learning rate $\eta$, initial parameters $\theta = (\mathbf{U}_z, \mathbf{W}_z, \mathbf{b}_z, \mathbf{U}_r, \mathbf{W}_r, \mathbf{b}_r\ \mathbf{U}_{\tilde{h}}, \mathbf{W}_{\tilde{h}}, \mathbf{b}_{\tilde{h}}, \mathbf{V}, \mathbf{b}_V)$.

**for** each epoch **do**
  Set $\phi = \phi_0$
  **for** t = 1 : T **do**
    Generate RLS input $\mathbf{x}_t$: $\mathbf{x}_t \leftarrow g(\mathbf{I}, \phi_{t-1})$
    Compute update gate $\mathbf{z}_t$, reset gate $\mathbf{r}_t$ and intermediate hidden unit $\tilde{\mathbf{h}}_t$:
    $\mathbf{z}_t \leftarrow \sigma(\mathbf{U}_z\mathbf{x}_t + \mathbf{W}_z\phi_{t-1} + \mathbf{b}_z)$
    $\mathbf{r}_t \leftarrow \sigma(\mathbf{U}_r\mathbf{x}_t + \mathbf{W}_r\phi_{t-1} + \mathbf{b}_r)$

$\tilde{\mathbf{h}}_t \leftarrow \tanh\left(\mathbf{U}_{\tilde{h}} x_t + \mathbf{W}_{\tilde{h}}(\phi_{t-1} \circ \mathbf{r}_t) + \mathbf{b}_{\tilde{h}}\right)$
Update the zero LS $\phi_t$: $\phi_t \leftarrow (1 - \mathbf{z}_t)\tilde{\mathbf{h}}_t + \mathbf{z}_t \phi_{t-1}$
**end for**
Compute the loss function $L$: $L \leftarrow -\sum_n \mathbf{y}_n \log \hat{\mathbf{y}}_n$
Compute the derivate w.r.t. $\theta$: $\nabla\theta \leftarrow \frac{\partial L}{\partial \theta}$.
Update $\theta$: $\theta \leftarrow \theta + \eta\nabla\theta$
**end for**

The proposed RLS described in the previous section performs the image segmentation task, i.e., dividing an image into two parts corresponding foreground and background segments. Given a real-world image, RLS however performs neither the instance segmentation nor image understanding which are significant tasks in many computer vision application. In order solve this requirement, we introduce contextual recurrent level sets (CRLS) for semantic object segmentation which is an extension of our proposed RLS model to address the multi-instance object segmentation in the wild. The proposed CRLS is able to (1) localize objects existing in the given image; (2) segment the objects out of the background; (3) classify the objects in the image. The output of our CRLS is multiple values (each value is corresponding to one object class) instead of two values (foreground and background) as in RLS.

Our proposed CRLS inherits the merits of RLS and faster-RCNN [12] for semantic segmentation which simultaneously performs three tasks which are addressed by three stages, i.e., detection, segmentation and classification in a fully end-to-end trainable framework as shown in **Figure 5**. In our CRLS, the network

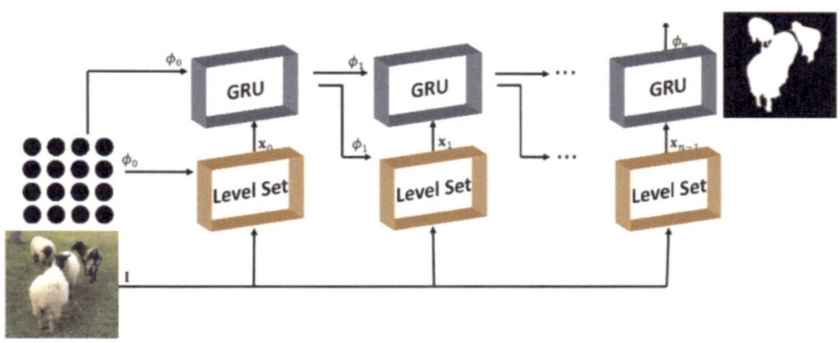


**Figure 4.**
*Visualization of relationship between LS and GRUs in a RLS unit.*

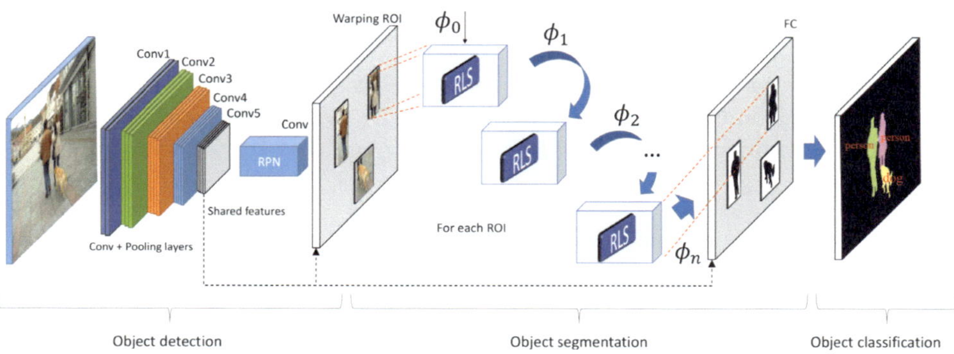


**Figure 5.**
*The flowchart of our proposed CRLS for semantic instance segmentation with three tasks which are addressed by three stages, i.e. object detection by Faster R-CNN [12], object segmentation by RLS and classiffication.*

takes an image of arbitrary size as the input, and outputs instance-aware semantic segmentation results. The network contains three components corresponding three stages of a semantic instance segmentation: object detection for proposing box-level, object segmentation is for mask-level and object classification is for categorizing each instance. These three stages are designed to share convolutional features. Each stage involves a loss term and the loss of later stage relies on the output of an predecessor stage, so the three loss terms are not independent. We train the entire network end-to-end with a unified loss function.

### 3.1 Stage 1: object detection

One of the most important approaches to the object detection and classification problems is the generations of region-based convolutional neural networks (R-CNN) family [12–15].

In order to propose a fully end-to-end trainable network, we adapt the region proposal network (RPN) introduced in Faster R-CNN [12] to predict the object bounding boxes and the objectness scores. Aiming at reducing time consuming, both the detection and segmentation procedure share the convolutional features of a deep VGG-16 network [16].

As for the share convolutional features, we utilize a VGG-16 networks with 13 convolution layers where each convolution layer is followed by a ReLU layer but only four pooling layers are placed right after the convolution layer to reduce the spatial dimension.

In this stage, object detection, the network proposes object instances in the form of bounding boxes which are predicted with an objectness score. The network structure and loss function of this stage follow the work of Region Proposal Networks (RPNs) [12]. RPNs take an image of any size as the input and predicts bounding box locations and objectness scores in a fully-convolutional form. A $3 \times 3$ convolutional layer for reducing the dimension is applied on top of share convolutional features. The lower dimension features are fed into two sibling $1 \times 1$ convolutional layers: one is for a box-regression layer and the other is for box-classification layer.

From the share feature maps and at each sliding-window location, multiple region proposals are generated. Denote $k$ is the maximum possible proposals for each location. Each box is presented by four values corresponding to locations (x, y w, h) and two scores corresponding the probability of object or not object. Each anchor, which is centered at the sliding window, is associated with an aspect ratio and scale. In the experiments, each sliding position has 9 (k = 9) anchors corresponding to three scales and three aspect ratios. If the sharing feature maps of size $W \times H$, there are $k \times W \times H$ anchors. For the purpose of object detection, there are only two anchors considered:

- *Positive anchor*: there are two cases are taken into account, i.e., (i) an anchor with the highest Intersection-over-Union (IoU) overlap with a ground-truth box, (ii) an anchor that has an IoU overlap higher than 0.7 with any ground-truth box.

- *Negative anchor*: an anchor with IoU score is lower than 0.3 with all ground-truth boxes.

- *Ignore anchor*: an anchor that is neither positive nor negative do not contribute to the training objective.

There are two sibling output layers: probability of classification and bounding box regression in the end of RPNs, therefore, the RPNs loss is based on two losses: boxes regression loss and object classification loss.

$$L_{RPN}\left(p^i, b^i\right) = \frac{1}{N_{cls}} \sum_i L_{cls}\left(p^i, p^{i*}\right) + \lambda \frac{1}{N_{reg}} \sum_i p^{i*} L_{reg}\left(b^i, b^{i*}\right) \tag{24}$$

In this equation:

- $i$ is the index of an anchor in a mini-batch.
- $p^i$ is the predicted probability of anchor $i$ being an object and $p^i$ is computed by a softmax over the $K$ outputs of a fully connected layer (K categories).
- $N_{cls}$ and $N_{reg}$ are the two normalization terms.
- $\lambda$ is a balancing parameter.
- $p^{i*}$ is groundtruth and it sets as 1 if the anchor is positive, and 0 if the anchor is negative.
- $b^i = \left(b_x^i, b_y^i, b_w^i, b_h^i\right)$ is a vector representing the four parameterized coordinates of the predicted bounding box.
- $b^{i*} = \left(b_x^{i*}, b_y^{i*}, b_w^{i*}, b_h^{i*}\right)$ is groundtruth bounding of positive box and is a vector representing the four parameterized coordinates. Let denote $(x^{i*}, y^{i*}, w^{i*}, h^{i*})$, $(x^i, y^i, w^i, h^i)$, $(x^a, y^a, w^a, h^a)$ are four coordinations (box center, width, and height) of groundtruth box, predicted box and anchor box, the parameterization of the four coordinates are as follows:

$$\begin{aligned} b_x^{i*} &= \left(x^{i*} - x^a\right)/w^a \quad & b_x^i &= \left(x^i - x^a\right)/w^a \\ b_y^{i*} &= \left(y^{i*} - y^a\right)/h^a \quad & b_y^i &= \left(y^i - y^a\right)/h^a \\ b_w^{i*} &= \log\left(w^{i*}/w^a\right) \quad & b_w^i &= \log\left(w^i/w^a\right) \\ b_h^{i*} &= \log\left(h^{i*}/h^a\right) \quad & b_h^i &= \log\left(h^i/h^a\right) \end{aligned} \tag{25}$$

- The bounding boxes regression is defined by $smooth_{l_1}$ as follows:

$$L_{reg} = \sum_{u \in x, y, w, h} smooth_{l_1}\left(b_u^i - b_u^{i*}\right) \tag{26}$$

$$smooth_{l_1}(x) = \begin{cases} \frac{1}{2}x^2 & if \quad |x| < 1 \\ |x| - 0.5 & otherwise \end{cases} \tag{27}$$

The classification loss ($L_{cls}$) is log loss over two classes (object vs. not object). The RPNs loss is defined as in Eq. (28) where $i$ is the ground truth class.

$$L_{cls}\left(p^i, p^{i*}\right) = -\log\left(p^i\right). \quad (28)$$

To easy to follow, we denote the loss of this stage as: $L_{RPN} = L_{RPN}(B(\Theta))$ where $\Theta$ represents all network parameters to be optimized. $B$ is the network output of this stage, representing a list of bounding boxes $B = \{b\}_i$. Each bounding box is presented by four coordinations (box center, width, and height) and predicted objectness probability $b_i = \left(b_x, b_y, b_w, b_h, p_i\right)_i$.

### 3.2 Stage 2: object segmentation

The second stage takes the share features and the results from the first stage (predicted box) as inputs. The output of this stage is binary segmentation which contains foreground (object) and background.

For each predicted box, we make use of RoI warping layer to crop and warp a region on the feature map into the target fixed size by interpolation. Each predicted box from the deep feature map (conv5) is now resized to $m \times m$ where $m = 21$ in our experiment. To reduce the size of a region, RoI warping layer is performed by using a pooling payer to convert features inside any valid region of interest into a small feature map. Each RoI is defined by top-left corner $(r, c)$ and its height and width $(h, w)$. That means, it is defined by a four-tuple $(r, c, h, w)$. The feature map of size $h \times w$ is partitioned into $m \times m$ grid of sub-windows of approximate size $\frac{h}{m} \times \frac{w}{m}$. The max pooling is then applied into each sub-window. As a result, RoI warping layer outputs a grid cell.

The fixed size extracted features are passed through the proposed RLS together with a randomly initial $\phi_0$ to generate a sequence input data $\mathbf{x}_t$ based on Eq. (18). The curve evolution procedure is performed via LS updating process given in Eqs. (14) and (17). This task outputs a binary mask as given in Eq. (23) sized $m \times m$ and parameterized by an $m^2$ dimensional vector.

Given a set of predicted bounding box from the first stage, the loss term $L_{SEG}$ of the second stage for foreground segmentation is given by:

$$L_{SEG} = L_{SEG}(S(\Theta)|B(\Theta)) \quad (29)$$

Here, $S$ is the network designed by RLS and is presenting a list of segmentations $S = \{S\}_i$. Each segmentation $S_i$ is an $m \times m$ mask.

### 3.3 Stage 3: object classification via fully-connected network

The third stage takes the share feature, bounding box from the first stage, object segmentation from the second stage as inputs. The output of this stage is class score for each object instance.

For each predicted bounding box from the first stage, we first extract the feature by ROI pooling ($f_{ROI}$). The feature is then go through the proposed RLS and presented by a binary mask ($f_{SEG}(\Theta)$) from the second stage. The input of this stage ($f_{MSK}$) is the masked feature which depends on the segmentation results ($f_{SEG}(\Theta)$) and ROI feature ($f_{ROI}$) and computed by element-wise product of those, $f_{MSK}(\Theta) = f_{ROI}(\Theta) * f_{SEG}(\Theta$. To predict the category of a region, we first apply two fully-connected layers to masked feature $f_{MSK}$. As a result, we receive mask-based feature vector which is then concatenated with another box-based feature vector to build a joined feature vector. Notably, the box-based feature vector is computed by applying two fully-connected layers to ROI feature $f_{ROI}$. Finally, two fully-connected layers are attached to the joined feature and each gives class scores and

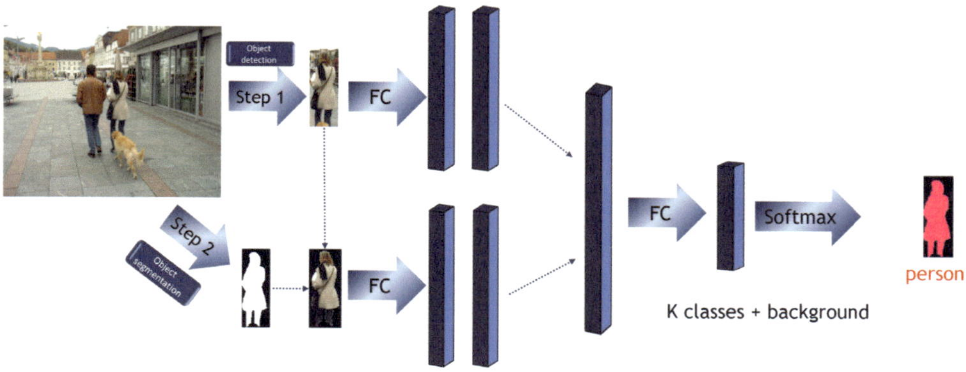


**Figure 6.**
*An illustration of Stage 3 for object classification using $f_{ROI}(\Theta) * f_{SEG}(\Theta)$ as inputs.*

refined bounding boxes using softmax classification of $(K + 1)$ classes (including background). The entire procedure of Stage 3 is illustrated in **Figure 6**.

Let $C$ is the network output of this stage and representing a list of category predictions for all instances: $C = \{C\}_i$. The loss term $L_{CLS}$ of the third stage is expressed in Eq. (30).

$$L_{CLS} = L_{CLS}(C(\Theta)|B(\Theta), S(\Theta)) \tag{30}$$

The loss of entire proposed CRLS network is defined as in Eq. (32).

$$\begin{aligned} L(\Theta) &= L_{RPN} + L_{SEG} + L_{CLS} \\ &= L_{RPN}(B(\Theta)) + L_{SEG}(S(\Theta)|B(\Theta)) + L_{CLS}(C(\Theta)|B(\Theta), S(\Theta)) \end{aligned} \tag{31}$$

## 4. Inference

In our experiment, the top-scored 300 ROIs are first chosen by RPNs proposed boxes giving an image. Using Non-maximum suppression (NMS) with IoU and threshold is chosen as 0.7 to filter out highly overlapping and redundant candidates. The proposed RLS is then applied on to each ROI to partition it into object (foreground) and non-object (background). From each ROI, we obtain a segmenting mask and a category score prediction via two fully-connected layers followed by a soft-max layer.

Besides softmax loss, which is to optimize when classifying a region is object or non-object in the first stage, there are three "dependent" losses in which the later loss depends on the predecessor loss. Three losses are assigned for each ROI, i.e., (1) smooth $l_1$ loss—bounding box regression loss in the first state, (2) cross entropy loss —foreground segmentation loss in the second stage (3) softmax loss—instance classification loss in the third stage. Among all the losses, computing the gradient w. r.t. predicted box positions and address the dependency on the bounding box $B(\Theta)$ is the most difficulty. Given a full size feature map $\mathcal{H}(\Theta)$, we crop a bounding box region (predicted box) $b_i(\Theta) = \left(b_x, b_y, b_w, b_h\right)$ and warp it to a fixed size by interpolation. The wrapped region ROI is presented as:

$$\mathcal{F}_{ROI}(\Theta) = \mathcal{I}(b_i(\Theta))\mathcal{F}(\Theta) \tag{32}$$

where $\mathcal{I}$ is cropping and warping operations. As for dimension, $\mathcal{F}(\Theta) \in \mathrm{R}^{\mathrm{N}}$ is a vector reshaped from the image, $N = W \times H$. The cropping and warping matrix

$\mathcal{I} \in \mathrm{R}^M \times \mathrm{R}^N$. $\mathcal{F}_{ROI}(\Theta)$ is a target region sized $w \times h$ and $M = w \times h$. $\mathcal{I}(b_i(\Theta))$ presents transforming a that box $b_i(\Theta)$ from size of $b_w \times b_h$ into the size of $w \times h$. Let $(x', y')$ and $(x, y)$ are two points on target feature map $\mathcal{F}_{ROI}(\Theta)$ size of $w \times h$ and original map $\mathcal{F}(\Theta)$ size of $(W \times H)$, respectively. Using interpolation with $(G)$ is the bilinear interpolation function, $\mathcal{I}(b_i(\Theta))$ is computed as follows:

$$\begin{aligned} \mathcal{I}(b_i(\Theta)) &= (G)\left(b_x + \frac{x'}{w} - x\right)(g)\left(b_y + \frac{y'}{h} - y\right) \\ g(z) &= \max(0, 1 - |z|) \end{aligned} \tag{33}$$

## 5. Implementation details

The proposed RLS approach is implemented using the TensorFlow system [17] whereas the extended CRLS semantic segmentation is implemented using Caffe environment [18]. Three functional sub-networks corresponding to three tasks, i.e., detection, segmentation and classification (shown in **Figure 5**), are connected together to construct an end-to-end network. The first and the third sub-networks, i.e., object detection and object classification, are adopted from Faster R-CNN framework [12]. In the second sub-network, we re-implement the defined layers from RLS-Tensorflow to RLS-Caffe for both forward and backward operations in Python. Since TensorFlow supports automatic differentiation capabilities, RLS-TensorFlow is therefore easier to implement than the new layers in RLS-Caffe.

In the experiment, the pre-trained VGG-16 model with 13 convolution layers is utilized to obtain the share features. Each convolution layer is always followed by a ReLU layer. There are 4 max-pooling layers are placed right after the convolution layer.

In the first task of CRLS, i.e., object detection, we use a $3 \times 3$ convolutional layer to reduce feature dimensions and learn the feature representation and then two consecutive $1 \times 1$ convolutional layers predicts object's locations and object's presenting scores. Furthermore, we choose the two normalization terms $(N_{cls}, N_{reg})$ are chosen as $N_{cls} = 256$ and $N_{reg} = 2400$. The balancing parameter $\lambda$ is set as $\lambda = 10$. As for non-maximum suppression (NMS), which is used to reduce the number of boxes generated from the first stage ($\sim 10^4$ regressed boxes are produced from the first stage), the threshold of the Intersection-over-Union (IoU) ratio is chosen as 0.7. As a result, the top-ranked 300 boxes are kept for the second stage.

In the second task of CRLS, i.e., object segmentation by the proposed RLS, we first extract a fixed-size ($21 \times 21$) deep feature from an arbitrary box predicted using the object detection task. The proposed RLS takes the extracted feature as the input together with the randomly initial $\phi_0$ to generate a sequence input data $x_t$ based on Eq. (18). The curve evolution procedure is performed via LS updating process given in Eq. (14). This task outputs a binary mask as given in Eq. (23) sized $m \times m$ and parameterized by an $m^2$ dimensional vector.

In the final task of CRLS, i.e., object classification, using the shared convolutional features inside the bounding box region, we extract a feature representation for each ROI. Through the second task of CRLS (object segmentation), we obtain the segmenting mask prediction for that ROI. The masked feature goes through two fully-connected layers to produce the classification score for that ROI.

The proposed CRLS framework was implemented on Caffe environment [18] and under SGD optimization. For each training image, if its shorter side is larger than 600, the image is down-scaled to 600 on the shorter side. To perform the experiments on PASCAL VOC [19], we train the network with 32 and 8 k iterations at learning rates of 0.001–0.0001, respectively. On the larger dataset like MSCOCO [20], we train the network with 180 and 20 k iterations at learning rates of 0.001–0.0001, respectively.

## 6. Experimental results of CRLS

In this section, we conduct two experiments corresponding to the object segmentation by the proposed RLS method and the semantic instance segmentation by the proposed CRLS system on PASCAL VOC [19] and COCO [20] datasets.

### 6.1 Datasets

#### *6.1.1 Synthetic dataset*

The synthetic and medical dataset containing 720 images are artificially created from images reported in [10, 21]. There are actually about 20 images reported in [10, 21]. To avoid over-fitting problem as well as make sure the proposed RLS is able to deal with both intensity homogeneity and inhomogeneity, different kinds of degradation and affined have been used. As for degradation, we use many kinds of noise and blurring at different ratio. As for affine transformations, we use rotation, translation, scale, and flip at different degrees. As a result, we obtain 720 images on this dataset. Half of this data set is used for training, i.e., 360 images which were artificially generated from first 10 images. The rest of 360 images is used for testing. Furthermore, we use the one object dataset from Weizmann [22] for the conducting the experiment on natural images. Using the same strategy of augmentation as in medical images, we obtain 4700 images and we used 2350 images for training and 2350 images for testing.

#### *6.1.2 PASCAL VOC*

The PASCAL VOC 2012 [19] are a commonly used database for evaluating semantic segmentation. The PASCAL VOC 2012 training and validation set has 11,540 images containing 27,450 bounding box annotated objects and 6929 segmentations in 20 categories and one background category. The data is divided into 5717 images for training and 5823 images for testing (val). The 20 object classes that have been selected are: person, bird, cat, cow, dog, horse, sheep, aeroplane, bicycle, boat, bus, car, motorbike, train, bottle, chair, dining table, potted plant, sofa, and tv/monitor.

#### *6.1.3 MS COCO*

The MS COCO training set contains about 80,000 images for training and 40,000 images for validation [20]. This dataset consists of ~500,000 annotated objects of 80 classes and one background class. COCO is a more challenging dataset as it contains objects in a wide range of scales from small ($<32^2$) to large ($>96^2$) objects.

### 6.2 Experiment 1: object segmentation by RLS

This section compares our object segmentation RLS against Chan-Vese's LS [10], DRLSE [23], Li's method. [24], L2S [25] and a simple Neural Network with two fully-connected layers followed by a ReLU layer in between and we name it

F-ConNet. The experiments are validated on both synthetic images, medical images and natural images collected in the wild. The input images are resized to $64 \times 64$, thus, the number of units in fully-connected layers and hidden cell of GRU is 4096.

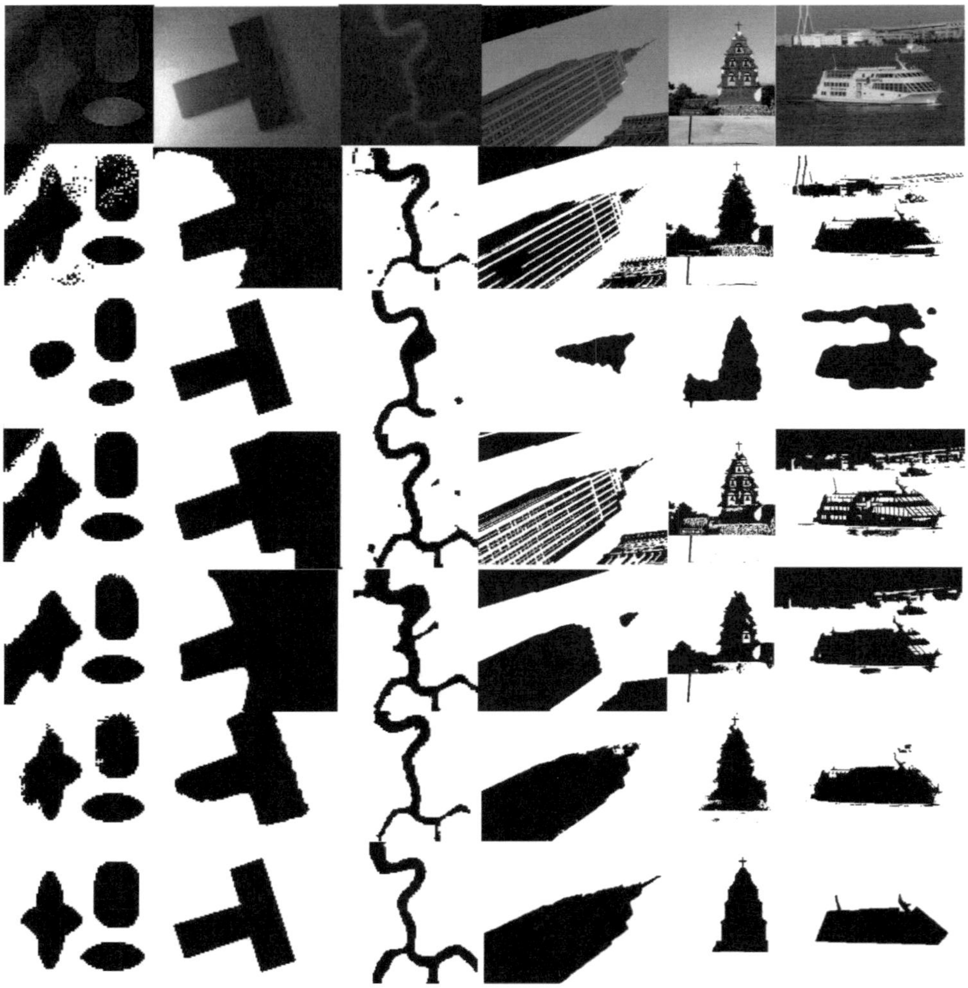

**Figure 7.**
*Comparison between the proposed RLS against other LS-based methods: $1^{st}$ row—input images, $2^{nd}$ row—CLS [10], $3^{rd}$ row—DRLSE [23], $4^{th}$ row—Li et al. [24], $5^{th}$ row—L2S [25], $6^{th}$ row—our RLS, and $7^{th}$ row—groundtruth. The best results for [10, 23–25].*

| Methods | FM (GT1) | FM (GT2) | Testing time |
|---|---|---|---|
| CV [10] | 88.51 | 87.51 | 13.5(s) |
| DRLSE [23] | 80.93 | 71.76 | 23.5(s) |
| Li et al. [24] | 79.65 | 63.87 | 20.4(s) |
| L2S [25] | 81.36 | 71.03 | 10.2(s) |
| F-ConNet | 93.30 | 93.26 | 0.001(s) |
| RLS | 99.16 | 99.17 | 0.008(s) |

**Table 2.**
*Average F-measure (FM) and testing time obtained by CV's model, DRLSE [23], Li et al. [24], L2S [25], F-ConNet and our proposed RLS with two different ground truth (GT1 and GT2) across Weizmann database.*

**Figure 7** shows comparison between our proposed RLS against other methods on image segmentation where CLS model [10] is used as baseline, DRLSE [23] as for global approach, Li et al. [24, 25], L2S [25] as for the inhomogeneity approach, F-ConNet as a baseline deep learning approach on the synthetic medical dataset and natural dataset. The best results from CLS's method, DRLSE, Li's method are L2S are given in the second, third, fourth, fifth rows respectively. The performance of our proposed RLS is given in the sixth row whereas the last row shows the ground truth. Quantity assessment on F-measure is given in **Table 2** with two separated

| Methods | $mAP^r$ @.5 | $mAP^r$ @.7 | Time (s) |
|---|---|---|---|
| SDS (AlexNet) | 49.7% | 25.3% | 48 |
| Hypercolumn | 60.0% | 40.4% | >80 |
| CFM | 60.7% | 39.6% | 32 |
| MNC | 63.5% | 41.5% | 0.36 |
| CRLS (Ours) | 66.7% | 44.6% | 0.54 |

**Table 3.**
*Quantitative results and comparisons against existing CNN-based semantic segmentation methods (SDS (AlexNet) [27], Hypercolumn [28], CFM [29], MNC [26]) on the PASCAL VOC 2012 validation set.*

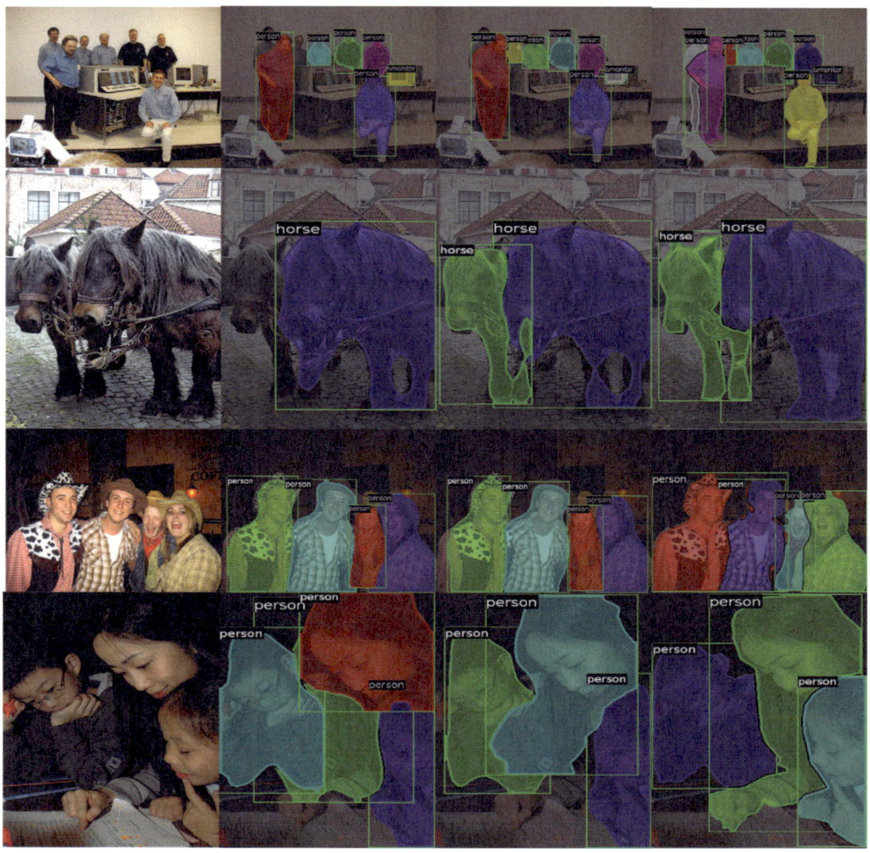

**Figure 8.**
*Some examples of semantic segmentation on PASCAL VOC 2012 database. The input image ($1^{st}$ column), MNC [25] ($2^{nd}$ column), our semantic segmentation CRLS ($3^{rd}$ column), and the ground truth ($4^{th}$ column) (best viewed in color).*

groundtruth versions (GT1 and GT2) provided by two different annotator on Weizmann database [22]. Compare to other methods, RLS achieves the best segmentation performance in this experiment on both groundtruth annotated by two different people.

In terms of time consuming, the baseline method CLS takes 13.5 s while Li et al.'s and DRLSE approaches have similar time consuming of 20.4 and 23.5 s on average to process one image with original size. L2S consumes less time (10.2 s) than the others CLS, Li's and DRLSE whereas the proposed RLS takes 0.008 s and F-ConNet takes least time consuming with 0.001 s.

**Figure 9.**
*Some examples of semantic segmentation on MS COCO database on validation set. The input image (1st column), MNC [26] our semantic segmentation CRLS (2nd column) and the ground truth (3rd column) (best viewed in color).*

| Methods | $mAP^r$ @[.5:.95] | $mAP^r$ @.5 |
|---|---|---|
| MNC | 19.5% | 39.7% |
| CRLS (Ours) | 20.5% | 40.1% |

**Table 4.**
*Quantitative results and comparisons against existing CNN-based semantic segmentation method MNC [26] on the MS COCO 2014 database.*

### 6.3 Experiment 2: semantic instance segmentation by CRLS

We demonstrate our proposed CRLS approach on two common semantic segmentation dataset, i.e., PASCAL VOC 2012 and MS COCO. The end-to-end CRLS network is trained using the ImageNet pre-trained VGG-16 model. We follow the same protocols used in recent papers [26–29] to evaluate the semantic segmentation task. We also use the same metrics reported in recent semantic object segmentation papers [26–29].

On PASCAL VOC dataset, we evaluate $mAP^r$ with IoU at 0.5 and 0.7. As shown in **Table 3**, we compare our proposed CRLS against state-of-the-art CNN-based semantic segmentation methods including SDS [27], Hypercolumn [28], CFM [29] and MNC [26]. As can be seen from the table, our CRLS achieves higher $mAP^r$ (about 3%) at both 0.5 and 0.7 than previous methods using the same testing protocol. Not only higher segmentation accuracy, the experimental results also show that our proposed CRLS gives very better testing time (0.54 second per image). Some illustrations of multi-instance object segmentation by our proposed CRLS on PASCAL VOC 2012 dataset are shown in **Figures 8** and **9**.

FOn MS COCO 2014, we use 80 k images for training and 20 k images in the test set (*test-dev*) for evaluating. The performance is measured on ($mAP^r$) using IoU between 0.5 and 0.95 and $mAP^r$ using IoU at 0.5 (as PASCAL VOC metrics). As shown in **Table 4**, our CRLS achieves better results than the previous method (MNC) on the COCO dataset.

## Author details

Thi Hoang Ngan Le[1*], Khoa Luu[1], Marios Savvides[2], Kha Gia Quach[3] and Chi Nhan Duong[3]

1 Department of Computer Science and Computer Engineering, University of Arkansas, Fayetteville AR, USA

2 Department of Electrical Computer Engineering, Carnegie Mellon University, Pittsburgh, PA, USA

3 PdActive Inc, Denver CO, USA

*Address all correspondence to: thihoanl@andrew.cmu.edu

## References

[1] LeCun Y, Touresky D, Hinton G, Sejnowski T. A theoretical framework for back-propagation. In: Proceedings of the 1988 Connectionist Models Summer School. CMU, Pittsburgh, PA: Morgan Kaufmann; 1988. pp. 21-28

[2] LeCun Y, Bottou L, Orr GB, Müller K-R. Efficient backprop. In: Neural Networks: Tricks of the Trade. Springer; 1998. pp. 9-50

[3] LeCun Y, Bottou L, Bengio Y, Haffner P. Gradient-based learning applied to document recognition. In: CVPR. 1998. pp. 2278-2324

[4] LeCun YL, Boser B, Denker JS, Howard RE, Habbard W, Jackel LD, Henderson D. Handwritten digit recognition with a back-propagation network. In: Nips. 1990. pp. 396-404

[5] Qian N. On the momentum term in gradient descent learning algorithms. Neural Networks. 1999;**12**(1):145-151

[6] Jordan MI. Attractor dynamics and parallelism in a connectionist sequential machine. In: Diederich J, editor. Artificial Neural Networks. 1990. pp. 112-127

[7] Rumelhart DE, Hinton GE, Williams RJ. Learning representations by back-propagating errors. In: Anderson JA, Rosenfeld E, editors. Neurocomputing: Foundations of Research. Cambridge, MA, USA: MIT Press; 1988. pp. 696-699

[8] Hochreiter S, Schmidhuber J. Long short-term memory. Neural Computation. 1997;**9**(8):1735-1780

[9] Cho K, van Merrienboer B, Gülçehre Ç, Bougares F, Schwenk H, Bengio Y. Learning phrase representations using RNN encoder-decoder for statistical machine translation. Computing Research Repository. 2014;**abs/1406**: 1078

[10] Chan TF, Vese LA. Active contours without edges. IEEE Transactions on Image Processing. 2001;**10**(2):266-277

[11] Mumford D, Shah J. Optimal approximation by piecewise smooth functions and associated Variational problems. Communications on Pure and Applied Mathematics. 1989;**42**(5): 577-685

[12] Ren S, He K, Girshick RB, Sun J. Faster R-CNN: Towards real-time object detection with region proposal networks. Computing Research Repository. 2015;**abs/1506**:01497

[13] Girshick R, Donahue J, Darrell JMT. Region-based convolutional networks for accurate object detection and semantic segmentation. Transactions on Pattern Analysis and Machine Intelligence. 2015;**38**:142-158

[14] Girshick R. Fast r-cnn. In: ICCV; 2015. pp. 1440-1448

[15] He K, Zhang X, Ren S, Sun J. Spatial pyramid pooling in deep convolutional networks for visual recognition. TPAMI. 2015;**37**(9):1904-1916

[16] Simonyan K, Zisserman A. Very deep convolutional networks for large-scale image recognition. arXiv preprint arXiv: 1409.1556. 2014

[17] Abadi M, Agarwal A, Barham P, Brevdo E, et al. TensorFlow: Large-scale machine learning on heterogeneous systems, software available from te nsorow.org. [Online]. 2015. Available from: http://tensorow.org/

[18] Jia Y, Shelhamer E, Donahue J, Karayev S, Long J, Girshick R, et al. Caffe: Convolutional architecture for fast feature embedding. In: ACM Intl. Conf. On Multimedia; 2014. pp. 675-678

[19] Everingham M, Van Gool L, Williams CKI, Winn J, Zisserman A. The pascal visual object classes (voc) challenge. International Journal of Computer Vision. 2010;**88**(2):303-338

[20] Lin T, Maire M, Belongie SJ, Bourdev LD, Girshick RB, Hays J, et al. Microsoft COCO: Common objects in context. Computing Research Repository. 2014;**abs/1405**:0312

[21] Li C, Kao CY, Gore JC, Ding Z. Minimization of region-scalable fitting energy for image segmentation. IEEE Transactions on Image Processing. 2008

[22] Alpert S, Galun M, Basri R, Brandt A. Image segmentation by probabilistic bottom-up aggregation and cue integration. In: CVPR; 2007

[23] Li C, Xu C, Gui C, Fox MD. Distance regularized level set evolution and its application to image segmentation. IEEE Transactions on Image Processing. 2010;**19**(12):3243-3254

[24] Li C, Huang R, Ding Z, Gatenby C, Metaxas DN, Gore JC. A level set method for image segmentation in the presence of intensity inhomogene ities with application to mri. IEEE Transactions on Image Processing. 2011; **20**(7):2007-2016

[25] Mukherjee S, Acton S. Region based segmentation in presence of intensity inhomogeneity using legendre polynomials. IEEE Signal Processing Letters. 2015;**22**(3):298-302

[26] Dai J, He K, Sun J. Instance-fully convolutional instance-aware semantic segmentation via multi-task network cascades

[27] Hariharan B, Arbeláez P, Girshick R, Malik J. Simultaneous detection and segmentation. In: European Conference on Computer Vision. Springer; 2014. pp. 297-312

[28] Hariharan B, Arbelaez P, Girshick R, Malik J. Hyper-columns for object segmentation and fine-grained localization. In: CVPR. 2015

[29] Dai J, He K, Sun J. Convolutional feature masking for joint object and stuff segmentation. In: CVPR; 2015. pp. 21

Chapter 5

# Pattern Recognition and Its Application in Solar Radiation Forecasting

*Mahmoud Ghofrani, Rasool Azimi and Mastaneh Youshi*

## Abstract

As intermittent renewable energy sources such as wind and solar proliferate, the power systems operation and planning become more complicated due to increased uncertainties and variabilities. Accurate forecasting of these sources facilitates planning and operating the electric grid to integrate wind/solar power more reliably and efficiently. The neural network learning process can be disrupted by anomalies of wind/solar time-series data, which results in less accurate forecasting. By processing and analyzing wind/solar time-series data, machine learning and pattern recognition methods such as data clustering and classification can significantly enhance the forecast accuracy. This chapter reviews the various machine learning and pattern recognition methods proposed in the literature for time-series forecasting of solar radiation.

**Keywords:** forecasting, pattern recognition, renewable energy, solar, time series

## 1. Introduction

Pattern recognition is the analysis of data to detect their patterns and arrangements [1]. Pattern recognition provides a signal identification technique that is popularly applied in time-series forecasting. Pattern recognition is particularly essential for highly fluctuating and volatile time series such as solar radiation with irregular patterns. The chaotic nature of solar radiation time-series data disrupts the neural network learning process and imposes high errors on forecasting. By better detecting anomalous data points (outliers) and irregular patterns, pattern recognition and machine learning-based techniques characterize the training data more accurately and provide better learning results for neural networks [2]. In this chapter, an overview of the most commonly used pattern recognition and machine learning methods for solar radiation forecasting is presented.

## 2. Pattern recognition methods in solar forecasting

Several pattern recognition methods have been used to identify patterns and provide a pattern-based prediction technique for solar irradiance [4, 6–8, 10, 13, 14, 16–21, 23–25]. A brief description is provided for each method in the following sections.

### 2.1 Combination of SOM, SVR, and PSO

Self-organizing map (SOM) is an unsupervised learning approach for data classification and clustering [2]. Support vector machines (SVMs) provide supervised learning for data classification and regression analysis [3]. Dong et al. [4] proposes a hybrid forecasting method combining SOM, support vector regression (SVR), and particle swarm optimization (PSO) methods. The SOM is used to divide the input space into disjointed regions with different characteristic information on the correlation between the input and the output. Then, the SVR is applied to model each disjointed region to identify the characteristic correlation. Finally, the PSO is applied to reduce the performance volatility of SVR with different parameters. The hybrid SOM-SVR-PSO method is rigorously tested and compared with several well-known time series forecasting algorithms. The comparison demonstrates higher accuracy of the proposed forecasting method.

### 2.2 Fuzzy c-means-based method

Fuzzy c-means (FCM) clustering is a well-known data clustering approach that allows each data element to belong to multiple clusters with varying degrees of membership [5]. Boata and Gravila [6] propose a novel method to forecast the stochastic component of the solar irradiation by the sky condition. By adopting the fuzzy inference system (FIS) principles, the proposed model forecasts daily clearness index. The FIS uses fuzzy logic to map any given input (features in the case of fuzzy clustering) to an output (clusters in the case of fuzzy clustering). In the proposed method, fuzzy c-means clustering is used to establish the membership functions (MFs) from the input variable's attributes. The MFs constitute the building blocks of the fuzzy set theory in fuzzy logic and characterize the fuzziness in a fuzzy set. The proposed method is evaluated and concluded to produce highly accurate results for practical applications.

### 2.3 Combination of fuzzy logic and neural networks

Fuzzy logic provides a powerful pattern recognition tool mainly because of its capability to characterize imperfect or noisy information and to measure data resemblance for clustering [7]. Chen et al. [8] proposes a new technique for solar radiation forecasting by combining the fuzzy logic and neural networks, to achieve a good accuracy at different conditions. In this method, the future sky conditions and temperature information are clustered to different fuzzy sets using a fuzzy logic-based clustering algorithm. The results demonstrate that the hybrid of fuzzy logic and neural network enhances the forecast accuracy for different sky and temperature conditions.

### 2.4 Spectral clustering

A new time-series clustering technique is proposed in Ref. [9] to reduce the computational complexity of smart grid optimization problems. Spectral clustering is used in this chapter to cluster different profiles for N days, where each day's profile is a time series over T slots. The data are clustered with respect to three different features including time attribute, frequency attribute, and weighted average of time-frequency attributes. The results show that clustering time-series data to provide two or more sub time series can improve the optimization performance when compared to using just a single typical time series.

### 2.5 Combination of k-means and NAR

K-means algorithm is a partition-based data clustering approach, which iteratively relocates data points among clusters for clustering optimization [10]. Nonlinear autoregressive (NAR) forecasting is based on the nonlinear relation between the past outputs and the predicted outputs, which and can be defined by a high-order diversity measure [11].

Benmouiza [12] proposes a hybrid of k-means clustering and NAR neural networks for short-term solar radiation forecasting. In this method, k-means algorithm is applied to extract useful information from the input data. By clustering the data, k-means recognizes patterns of the input space, which provides better training for the neural network and improves the forecasting results. The proposed hybrid method first uses the mutual information (MI) approach to identify the suitable time delay and reconstitutes the phase space of solar radiation time series. The false nearest neighbors (FNN) algorithm is then used to determine the minimum embedding dimension for reconstructing the nonlinear dynamics from a time series. The next phase involves the k-means clustering to cluster the input patterns into k groups with similar characteristics. The silhouette method is applied to select the most suitable number of clusters. A NAR neural network is then trained for each cluster as a sub-predictor for the corresponding subset of the input pattern. Finally, another NAR network is applied as a global predictor for the solar radiation time-series data. Taking advantage of both k-means and NAR, the proposed forecasting method provides satisfactory results.

### 2.6 K-fold-based method

K-fold cross validation approach is a resampling procedure used to evaluate machine learning models over a sample data. The bootstrap is another resampling technique that generates multiple datasets by sampling from the original single dataset [13]. A combination of bootstrap sampling, k-fold cross validation, mutual information, and stationary time-series processing with clear sky model is applied in Ref. [13] for solar radiation forecasting. In this method, the cumulative distribution function (CDF) and matching quintile estimation (MQE) are used to determine the prediction interval. Based on the evaluation results, the proposed method demonstrates higher accuracy for forecasting horizons varying between 1 and 6 hours.

### 2.7 Combination of ANN with fuzzy logic pre-processing

Sivaneasan [14] develops an improved solar forecasting algorithm by combining fuzzy logic pre-processing and artificial neural network (ANN) model. The fuzzy pre-processing is used to calculate the correlation between temperature, cloud cover, wind speed, and direction with irradiance values. In this method, a three-layer feed forward with back-propagation model is applied as the neural network training algorithm. An error correction factor is proposed to reduce forecast errors by combining the error from the previous 5-min estimated output in the input layer. The evaluation results demonstrate that the error correction factor combined with the ANN approach improves solar irradiance forecasting accuracy due to its adaptive error correction capability. The forecasting accuracy of the proposed method is compared with other ANN forecasting algorithms. The results show that the proposed method has a better performance.

## 2.8 Semi-empirical methods

Ångström-Prescott (AP) is a model used to estimate the global solar irradiation as a function of solar radiation at the earth's surface and daily sunshine duration [15]. Akarslan et al. [16] presents five semi-empirical solar radiation forecasting models based on the AP approach. These models utilize solar irradiance historical data along with the extra-terrestrial irradiance and the clearness index for hourly forecasting of solar radiation. Models 1–2 use historical samples of solar radiation and clearness index, whereas models 3–5 utilize the extra-terrestrial irradiance in addition to historical values of solar radiation and clearness index. The evaluation results show that including the extra-terrestrial irradiance data in the model enhances the forecasting accuracy.

## 2.9 Combination of k-means, DT, and SVM-C

A hybrid framework is proposed in Ref. [17] to model and forecast hourly global solar radiation data. This approach includes two different phases and uses data mining techniques in each step. K-means clustering technique is used in the first phase to identify the type of days. In the second phase, the decision trees (DT), artificial neural networks, support vector machine regression (SVM-R), and support vector machine classification algorithms (SVM-C) are combined with regression algorithms to obtain the daily clearness index and the meteorological parameters to forecast hourly global solar radiation. The results of the evaluation indicate that the proposed method satisfies the desired accuracy.

## 2.10 Machine learning-based methods

Five machine learning models, including adaptive forward-backward greedy algorithm (Fo-Ba), leap-Forward, forecast and variable selection by spike and slab regression (spikeslab), bagging wrapper for multivariate adaptive regression splines (Bagged MARS) using generalized cross validation (gCV) pruning, Cubist, and bagEarthGCV are presented in Ref. [18] for the solar irradiance prediction. The Fo-Ba algorithm is an efficient sparse learning and feature selection method with applications in optimization problems. The spikeslab model is a prediction and variable selection approach based on spike and slab regression. Bagged MARS approach computes an Earth model for each bootstrap sample of the original training set. In addition, the generalized cross validation approach is used for regularizing parameter selection in geophysical diffraction tomography (GDT). The above-mentioned models are evaluated and compared for different forecasting horizons from 1 h ahead to 48 h ahead. The evaluation results show that the spikeslab and Cubist models have more accurate and consistent performance for different forecasting horizons.

## 2.11 Combination of SOM and wavelet neural networks

Wavelet neural network is the combination of wavelet analysis and neural networks to address the over fitting issue of single network models. Reference [19] develops a novel short-term PV generation forecasting method by combining SOM algorithm and wavelet neural networks. The SOM method is applied for clustering the weather data and recognizing the future weather type. The wavelet neural network is utilized to build the prediction models for each cluster sample. The proposed method is proven to culminate in highly accurate forecasting.

### 2.12 Adaptive neuro-fuzzy system

Mohammadi et al. [20] propose an adaptive neuron-fuzzy inference system (ANFIS)-based model for daily solar radiation forecasting. The ANFIS method is a hybrid artificial intelligence method combining learning and generalization ability of neural network with characteristics of fuzzy inference system. The results demonstrate that the ANFIS model is an effective approach in the field of solar radiation forecasting.

### 2.13 SVR-based method

Support vector regression (SVR) is a variant of SVM that is used to compute the linear regression function of a nonlinear mapping [3]. SVR methodology is used in Ref. [21] for horizontal global solar radiation forecasting based on the daily hours of sunshine and daylight. The obtained results show that this method forecasts the monthly average daily global solar radiation with higher accuracy over the PSO-based models.

### 2.14 Combination of SVM, WT, ANN, and GA methods

Wavelet transform (WT) is a time-series analysis tool that decomposes a signal into a representation demonstrating time-series details and trends as a function of time [22]. Mohammadi et al. [23] uses a hybrid of support vector machine and wavelet transform algorithm (SVM-WT) for extracting features of solar radiation data. In addition, the artificial neural network (ANN) and genetic algorithm (GA) are combined to forecast daily global solar radiation. The results show that the SVM-WT method improves the forecasting accuracy by recognizing the patterns and providing better training for the neural network.

### 2.15 Clustering-based multi-model method

Wu and Chan [24] propose a novel multi-model framework for solar radiation forecasting. The framework is based on the assumption that there are several patterns in the stochastic component of solar radiation series. The time series data are first classified into multiple subsequences. The k-means algorithm is then applied to group the subsequence into different clusters. Finally, the time-delay neural network (TDNN) is trained to model a specific pattern in each cluster. The pattern corresponding to the current time is then determined for the forecasting purpose. This process is followed by selecting the appropriate trained TDNN model. The comparison analysis of the proposed forecasting method with autoregressive-moving-average (ARMA) model shows that the proposed model provides superior performance.

### 2.16 Data-driven method

Aerosol Optical Depth (AOD) and the Angstrom Exponent data are used in [25] and are included in several data-driven models for hourly solar radiation forecasting. Several machine learning methods including multilayer perceptron (MLP), SVR, k-nearest neighbors (kNN), and decision tree regression are used as the data-driven models and evaluated for their forecasting accuracies. The evaluation results show that the MLP method outperforms other data-driven forecasting models.

## 3. Performance metrics

Several indexes are presented for evaluating the performance of time-series prediction methods. These indexes are used to represent the forecast error. Lower error values correspond to more accurate forecasting. This section provides the definitions and mathematical representations for most commonly used error indexes in forecasting.

Note that $S_{Actual}$ is the observed value, $\hat{S}$ is the predicted value (forecast), and $N$ is the total number of observations.

### 3.1 MSE

The mean square error (MSE) is used as the accuracy performance indicator given by:

$$\mathrm{MSE} = \frac{1}{N}\sum_{n=1}^{N}\left(\hat{S}(n) - S_{Actual}(n)\right)^2 \tag{1}$$

### 3.2 nMSE

Normalized mean square error (nMSE) is an estimator of overall deviations between the forecasted and measured samples. It is defined as follows:

$$\mathrm{nMSE} = \frac{N\sum_{n=1}^{N}\left(\hat{S}(n) - S_{Actual}(n)\right)^2}{\sum_{n=1}^{N}\hat{S}(n).\sum_{n=1}^{N}S_{Actual}(n)} \tag{2}$$

### 3.3 RMSE

The square root of MSE is given by:

$$\mathrm{RMSE} = \sqrt{\frac{1}{N}\sum_{n=1}^{N}\left(\hat{S}(n) - S_{Actual}(n)\right)^2} \tag{3}$$

### 3.4 nRMSE

Normalized root mean square error (NRMSE) is calculated as follows:

$$\mathrm{nRMSE} = \frac{\sqrt{\frac{1}{N}\sum_{n=1}^{N}\left(\hat{S}(n) - S_{Actual}(n)\right)^2}}{\frac{1}{N}\sum_{n=1}^{N}S_{Actual}(n)} \tag{4}$$

### 3.5 MAE

Mean absolute error is calculated as follows:

$$\mathrm{MAE} = \frac{1}{N}\sum_{n=1}^{N}\left|\hat{S}(n) - S_{Actual}(n)\right| \tag{5}$$

### 3.6 nMAE

Normalized mean absolute error (nMAE) is given by:

$$\text{nMAE} = \frac{1}{N}\sum_{n=1}^{N}\frac{\left|\hat{S}(n) - S_{Actual}(n)\right|}{\max(S_{Actual}(n))} \tag{6}$$

### 3.7 MAPE

Mean absolute percentage error is calculated as follows:

$$\text{MAPE} = \frac{1}{N}\sum_{n=1}^{N}\left|\frac{\hat{S}(n) - S_{Actual}(n)}{S_{Actual}(n)}\right| \tag{7}$$

### 3.8 MBE

Mean bias error (MBE) is given by:

$$\text{MBE} = \frac{1}{N}\sum_{n=1}^{N}\hat{S}(n) - S_{Actual}(n) \tag{8}$$

### 3.9 nMBE

Normalized mean bias error (nMBE) is calculated by normalizing the MBE as follows:

$$\text{nMBE} = \frac{\sum_{n=1}^{N}\hat{S}(n) - S_{Actual}(n)}{\sum_{n=1}^{N}S_{Actual}(n)} \tag{9}$$

### 3.10 MABE

The MABE represents the mean absolute bias error as follows:

$$\text{MABE} = \frac{1}{N}\sum_{n=1}^{N}\left|\hat{S}(n) - S_{Actual}(n)\right| \tag{10}$$

### 3.11 SMAPE

The SMAPE represents symmetric mean absolute percentage error as follows:

$$\text{SMAPE} = \frac{1}{N}\sum_{n=1}^{N}\frac{\left|\hat{S}(n) - S_{Actual}(n)\right|}{\left(\hat{S}(n) + S_{Actual}(n)\right)^{2}} \times 100 \tag{11}$$

### 3.12 Forecast skill

The forecast skill is an error index which provides accuracy comparison between any given forecasting model and the persistence forecasting method. The forecast skill is calculated by:

$$\text{Forecast Skill} = \left(1 - \frac{\text{RMSE}}{\text{RMSE (Persistence)}}\right) \tag{12}$$

A forecast skill of 1.0 implies an unattainable perfect forecasting, and a forecast skill of 0.0 indicates a performance similar to the persistence method. Besides, negative values show lower forecasting accuracies compared to the persistence method. Detailed explanations and applications of the forecast skill can be found in [26].

**Table 1** provides a summary of the solar radiation forecasting methods explained in subsections 2.1–2.16, along with the error metrics used for each method.

| References | Forecast variable | Forecast horizon | Error metric | Method | Data |
|---|---|---|---|---|---|
| [4] | Hourly GHI* | 1 h | nRMSE, nMBE | Hybrid SOM-SVR-PSO | Colorado, USA and South Park, Singapore |
| [6] | Daily global solar irradiation | 1 day | RMSE, MBE | Functional fuzzy approach | World Radiation Data Center (WRDC), St. Petersburg, Russia |
| [7] | Hourly solar radiation | 1 h | MAPE | Hybrid of fuzzy logic and neural networks | National Environment Agency (NEA) |
| [8] | Hourly solar radiation | 1 h | nRMSE, MAPE | A decomposition-clustering-ensemble learning approach | Beijing, China |
| [10] | Hourly solar radiation | 1 h | RMSE, nRMSE | Hybrid k-means-NAR | National Meteorological Office of Algeria for the site of Oran |
| [13] | Hourly GHI | 1 h | nRMSE, forecast skill | Combination of bootstrap sampling, k-fold approach, mutual information, and stationary processing | Global Earth Observation System of Systems (GEOSS) |
| [14] | Very short term GHI | 5-min | MAPE | Combination of ANN with fuzzy logic pre-processing | Singapore |
| [16] | Hourly solar radiation | 1 h | MBE, RMSE, nRMSE | AP-based semi-empirical models | Solar observation station at Afyon Kocatepe University |
| [17] | Hourly GHI | 1 h | MAE, rMAE, nRMSE | Combination k-means, DT and SVM-C | Photovoltaic Systems Laboratory of the University of Malaga |
| [18] | Hourly solar radiation | 1 h–48 h | RMSE | Machine learning-based models | National renewable energy laboratory (NREL) |
| [19] | Daily global solar irradiation | 1 day | nMAPE, nRMSE | Combination of SOM and wavelet neural networks | Zhejiang Global Photovoltaic Technology |

| References | Forecast variable | Forecast horizon | Error metric | Method | Data |
|---|---|---|---|---|---|
| [20] | Daily global solar irradiation | 1 day | RMSE, MAPE | ANFIS-based approach | Tabas County, South Khorasan Province, Iran |
| [21] | Daily global solar irradiation | 1 day | RMSE, MAPE, MABE | SVR-based methodology | Arid desert cold climate of Isfahan, Iran |
| [23] | Daily global solar irradiation | 1 day | RMSE, MAPE, MABE | Hybrid SVM-WT-ANN-GA | Bandar Abbas, Iran |
| [24] | Hourly solar radiation | 1 h | SMAPE, RMSE | Clustering-based multi-model method | Nanyang Technological University, Singapore |
| [25] | Hourly GHI/ DNI**/ DHI*** | 1 h | RMSE, forecast skill | Machine learning-based data-driven models | Saudi Arabia |

*Global horizontal irradiance (GHI).
**Direct normal irradiance (DNI).
***Diffuse horizontal irradiance (DHI).

**Table 1.**
*Summary of the pattern recognition-based solar forecasting methods.*

## 4. Conclusion

This chapter provides a comprehensive literature review to demonstrate the application of pattern recognition and machine learning techniques for solar radiation forecasting. The results of this survey show that identifying the irregular patterns of solar radiation time series by data clustering and/or classification provides better training for neural networks and enhances the forecast accuracy. However, computational complexities of hybrid forecasting methods utilizing multiple pattern recognition and machine learning techniques render their applications inefficient for online predictions or very short-term forecasting.

## Author details

Mahmoud Ghofrani[1*], Rasool Azimi[2] and Mastaneh Youshi[3]

1 School of Science, Technology, Engineering and Mathematics (STEM), University of Washington, Bothell, USA

2 Young Researchers and Elite Club, Qazvin Branch, Islamic Azad University, Qazvin, Iran

3 Faculty of Computer and Information Technology Engineering, Qazvin Branch, Islamic Azad University, Qazvin, Iran

*Address all correspondence to: mrani@uw.edu

## References

[1] Ferreira AMS, Cavalcante CAMT, Fontes CHO, Marambio JES. 5.14 Patterns recognition in energy management. In: Dincer I, editor. Comprehensive Energy Systems. Oxford: Elsevier; 2018. pp. 537-580

[2] Engelbrecht AP. Computational Intelligence: An Introduction. Hoboken, New Jersey, United States: Wiley Publishing, Books, Academic Journals; 2007

[3] Cortes C, Vapnik V. Support-vector networks. Machine Learning. 1995; **20**(3):273-297

[4] Dong Z, Yang D, Reindl T, Walsh WM. A novel hybrid approach based on self-organizing maps, support vector regression and particle swarm optimization to forecast solar irradiance. Energy. 2015;**82**:570-577

[5] Bezdek JC, Ehrlich R, Full W. FCM: The fuzzy C-means clustering algorithm. Computers & Geosciences. 1984;**10**(2–3):191-203

[6] Boata RS, Gravila P. Functional fuzzy approach for forecasting daily global solar irradiation. Atmospheric Research. 2012;**112**:79-88

[7] Schmalzel JL, Johnson JF. Pattern Recognition Based on Fuzzy Logic. Paper presented at the 1993 IEEE Instrumentation and Measurement Technology Conference; 18–20 May 1993

[8] Chen SX, Gooi HB, Wang MQ. Solar radiation forecast based on fuzzy logic and neural networks. Renewable Energy. 2013;**60**:195-201

[9] Sun S, Wang S, Zhang G, Zheng J. A decomposition-clustering-ensemble learning approach for solar radiation forecasting. Solar Energy. 2018;**163**: 189-199

[10] Lloyd SP. Least squares quantization in PCM. IEEE Transactions on Information Theory. 1982;**28**(2):129-136

[11] Pawlus W, Karimi HR, Robbersmyr KG. Data-based modeling of vehicle collisions by nonlinear autoregressive model and feedforward neural network. Information Sciences. 2013;**235**:65-79. DOI: 10.1016/j.ins.2012.03.013

[12] Benmouiza K, Cheknane A. Forecasting hourly global solar radiation using hybrid k-means and nonlinear autoregressive neural network models. Energy Conversion and Management. 2013;**75**:561-569

[13] Voyant C, Motte F, Notton G, Fouilloy A, Nivet M-L, Duchaud J-L. Prediction intervals for global solar irradiation forecasting using regression trees methods. Renewable Energy. 2018; **126**:332-340

[14] Sivaneasan B, Yu CY, Goh KP. Solar forecasting using ANN with fuzzy logic pre-processing. Energy Procedia. 2017; **143**:727-732

[15] Paulescu M, Stefu N, Calinoiu D, Paulescu E, Pop N, Boata R, et al. Ångström–Prescott equation: Physical basis, empirical models and sensitivity analysis. Renewable and Sustainable Energy Reviews. 2016;**62**:495-506

[16] Akarslan E, Hocaoglu FO, Edizkan R. Novel short term solar irradiance forecasting models. Renewable Energy. 2018;**123**:58-66

[17] Jiménez-Pérez PF, Mora-López L. Modeling and forecasting hourly global solar radiation using clustering and classification techniques. Solar Energy. 2016;**135**:682-691

[18] Sharma A, Kakkar A. Forecasting daily global solar irradiance generation using machine learning. Renewable and

Sustainable Energy Reviews. 2018;**82**: 2254-2269

[19] Yang Y, Dong L. Short-term PV generation system direct power prediction model on wavelet neural network and weather type clustering. Paper presented at the Proceedings of the 2013 5th International Conference on Intelligent Human-Machine Systems and Cybernetics–Volume 01; 2013

[20] Mohammadi K, Shamshirband S, Tong CW, Alam KA, Petković D. Potential of adaptive neuro-fuzzy system for prediction of daily global solar radiation by day of the year. Energy Conversion and Management. 2015;**93**:406-413

[21] Mohammadi K, Shamshirband S, Anisi MH, Alam KA, Petković D. Support vector regression based prediction of global solar radiation on a horizontal surface. Energy Conversion and Management. 2015;**91**:433-441

[22] Kumar A, Komaragiri R, Kumar M. Design of wavelet transform based electrocardiogram monitoring system. ISA Transactions. 2018

[23] Mohammadi K, Shamshirband S, Tong CW, Arif M, Petković D, Ch S. A new hybrid support vector machine–wavelet transform approach for estimation of horizontal global solar radiation. Energy Conversion and Management. 2015;**92**:162-171

[24] Wu J, Chan CK. Prediction of hourly solar radiation with multi-model framework. Energy Conversion and Management. 2013;**76**:347-355

[25] Alfadda A, Rahman S, Pipattanasomporn M. Solar irradiance forecast using aerosols measurements: A data driven approach. Solar Energy. 2018;**170**:924-939

[26] Inman RH, Pedro HT, Coimbra CF. Solar forecasting methods for renewable energy integration. Progress in Energy and Combustion Science. 2013;**39**(6): 535-576

Chapter 6

# Diagnosis of Skin Lesions Based on Dermoscopic Images Using Image Processing Techniques

*Ihab Zaqout*


## Abstract

Great effort has been put into the development of diagnosis methods for the most dangerous type of skin diseases—melanoma. This paper aims to develop a prototype capable of segment and classify skin lesions in dermoscopy images based on ABCD rule. The proposed work is divided into four distinct stages: (1) pre-processing, consists of filtering and contrast enhancing techniques, (2) segmentation, thresholding, and statistical properties are computed to localize the lesion, (3) features extraction, asymmetry is calculated by averaging the calculated results of the two methods: entropy and bi-fold. Border irregularity is calculated by accumulate the statistical scores of the eight segments of the segmented lesion. Color feature is calculated among the existence of six candidate colors: white, black, red, light-brown, dark-brown, and blue-gray. Diameter is measured by the conversion operation from the total number of pixels in the greatest diameter into millimeter (mm), and (4) classification, the summation of the four extracted feature scores multiplied by their weights to yield a total dermoscopy score (TDS); hence, the lesion is classified into benign, suspicious, or malignant. The prototype is implemented in MATLAB and the dataset used consists of 200 dermoscopic images from Hospital Pedro Hispano, Matosinhos. The achieved results show an acceptable performance rates, an accuracy 90%, sensitivity 85%, and specificity 92.22%.


**Keywords:** dermoscopy, ABCD rule, segmentation, feature extraction, classification

## 1. Introduction

Melanoma, also known as malignant melanoma, is the most dangerous type of skin cancer that progresses from the pigment-containing cells known as melanocytes. Sometimes they progress from a mole with concerning changes including an increase in size, irregular edges, and change in color, itchiness, or skin breakdown [1]. Melanomas may rarely occur in the mouth, intestines, or eye but typically occur in the skin [1, 2]. In men, they most commonly occur on the back, while in women, they are most common on the legs [2].

Authors of [2] also mentioned that the ultraviolet light (UV) exposure from either the sun or from other sources, such as tanning devices is the primary cause of melanoma, while about 25% develop from moles. Worldwide, in 2012, it registered 55,000 death cases in 232,000 people. North America, Europe, Australia, and New

Zealand have the highest rates of melanoma in the world while it is less common in Latin America, Asia, and Africa.

One of the widely used methods by dermatologists to classify the cancerous skin —melanoma from normal skin is the ABCD rule. It is proved that it can be easily learned and rapidly calculated and has been proven to be a reliable method providing a more objective and reproducible diagnosis of melanoma [3–5]. To calculate the ABCD score, the "asymmetry, border, colors, and diameter" criteria are approximately estimated (semi-quantitatively). Each of the criteria is then multiplied by a given weight factor to yield a total dermoscopy score (TDS). TDS values less than 4.75 indicate a benign melanocytic lesion, values between 4.8 and 5.45 indicate a suspicious lesion, and values of 5.45 or greater are highly suggestive of melanoma.

To calculate the Asymmetry, the melanocytic lesion is bisected by two 90° axes. If both axes dermoscopically show asymmetric contours with regard to shape, the asymmetry score is 2. If there is asymmetry on one axis only, the score is 1. If asymmetry is absent with regard to both axes the score is 0. The border is calculated by dividing the lesion into eighths. Within each one-eighth, a sharp, abrupt cut-off of pigment pattern at the periphery receives a score 1, otherwise receives a score 0. Color feature is calculated by counting the existence of six different colors: white, red, light brown, dark brown, blue-gray, and black. The Diameter of melanomas is usually greater than 6 mm.

The proposed work relies on extracting and selecting specific information features that can be used to distinguish malignant, suspicious, and benign lesions by setting an automated cancer diagnosis using image processing techniques. More details on the image processing techniques used in this research exist in [6].

To achieve the aim of this research, four stages are implemented sequentially:

- Pre-processing stage: it consists of filtering and contrast enhancement techniques to remove any unwanted structures (i.e., hair) that might corrupt the image. Also the aim of this stage is to eliminate the background noise and improve the image quality for the purpose of determining the focal areas in the image.

- Segmentation stage: thresholding for binarization and statistical properties are computed such as, area and center of mass to localize the lesion.

- Feature extraction/selection stage: this stage quantifies the ABCD rule. Asymmetry feature is calculated by averaging produced results from the two methods: Entropy and Bi-fold. Border irregularity is measured by the partition of the skin's lesion into eight equal segments, the segment's perimeter and area is calculated for each segment, and then accumulating their scores. Color feature is calculated among the existence of six candidate colors: white, black, red, light-brown, dark-brown, and blue-gray. Diameter is measured by the conversion operation from the total number of pixels in the greatest diameter into millimeter (mm).

- The classification of image: this stage depends on the summation of the four extracted feature scores multiplied by their weights to yield a total dermoscopy score (TDS). Based on the TDS, the lesion is classified into benign, suspicious, or malignant.

Section 2 describes an overview of several systems proposed in the literature. Section 3 describes the research methodology. The experimental study and discussion are described in Section 4. Section 5 concludes this paper with some remarks on future work.

## 2. Related works

Several diagnostic systems for melanoma detection have been proposed. Some systems try to imitate the performance of dermatologists by detecting and extracting several dermoscopic features. These features can then be used to score a lesion in a similar way to the one adopted by dermatologists. In [7], general clinical principles of early melanoma detection are reviewed, providing the clinician with an up-to-date understanding of management strategies for their patients with numerous or atypical nevi. Many researchers have been working on the image processing and computer vision techniques for skin cancer detection. The most probably features to perform skin lesion segmentation used in various papers are shape, color, texture, and luminance.

Three methods of segmentation have been discussed by [8]. The methods are: Otsu's method, gradient vector flow (GVF), and color based using K-mean clustering. Feature extraction is based on the so-called ABCD-rule of dermatoscopy. While [9], a watershed segmentation is the proposed scheme used for image segmentation, border detection and decision related with structural nature of lesion. For more details of study, the segmentation methods used, a survey work on skin lesion segmentation problem implemented by image processing techniques are described by [10–12].

Based on a qualitative assessment of asymmetry (of boundary, color, and mass distribution), size functions (SFs) and support vector machine (SVM) are used to implement a new automatic classifier of melanocytic lesions [13]. An automatic identification of asymmetry in digital images containing melanocytic skin lesion using Stolz strategy, based on the ABCD rule is proposed by [14]. A survey on asymmetry analysis of malignant melanoma using image processing techniques to identify the asymmetricity of the melanoma skin lesions was presented by [15].

Several researchers proposed an image analysis tools to check for the various melanoma parameters like asymmetry, border, color, diameter, in terms of texture, size, and shape analysis for image segmentation and feature stages. The extracted feature parameters are used to classify the image as normal skin and melanoma cancer lesion [16–22].

In [23], they applied a Bag-of-features approach to malignant melanoma detection based on epiluminescence microscopy imaging (low-power microscopy (×50–100), commonly a television microscope applied to a glass slide covering mineral oil on the surface of a skin lesion, to determine malignancy in pigmented lesions). Each skin lesion is represented by a histogram of code words or clusters identified from a training data set. Classification results are achieved based on the implementation of naive Bayes and support vector machine classifiers. Other work utilized the Bag-of-feature model for the detection of melanomas in dermoscopy images and aimed at identifying the role of different local texture and color descriptors [24]. The reported results show that the sensitivity is 93% and specificity is 85%.

The extracted features of segmented lesions used as inputs to the input layer of the artificial neural network. Different configurations of ANNs were implemented by the researchers for classification [25–28]. In [25], they attached the Dermlite® DL1 dermatoscope to the iPhone. A new method called elliptical symmetry was proposed for quantifying asymmetry. Gaussian smoothing and lacunarity analysis to measure border irregularity were proposed. In Gaussian smoothing, the contour was smoothed and compared with the perimeter of the original lesion. The lacunarity was used to analysis the borders of the image. Finally, the extracted features were fed to input layer of the multi-stage neural network classifier. While [26], 2D-Wavelet transform is the feature extraction method used. These features are given as the input to the artificial neural network classifier. An unsupervised approach for lesion segmentation is proposed by [27]. Iterative thresholding is applied to initialize level set automatically. The accuracy of detected border is compared with Growcut and mean-shift algorithms. Four features relying on visual diagnosis: asymmetry (A), border (B), color (C), and diameter (D) are computed and used to construct a classification module based on artificial neural network for the recognition of malignant melanoma. The authors of [28] used a hybrid algorithm combining a region-oriented and a thresholding method to segment the lesion. A multilayer perceptron NN model with one hidden layer and one output neuron was chosen as a basis for all the different network configurations examined.

As described by [29], the general approach used by a CAD system consists in describing the skin lesion by means of a set of textural and geometrical shape features known as the ABCD rule (asymmetry, border, color and diameter). Software WEKA was used to apply 13 different techniques and a statistical test K-folds to obtain the classification accuracy.

A different approach proposed by [30] named Modified Texture Distinctiveness Lesion Segmentation algorithm (M-TDLS) to segment the skin lesion. Two steps are involved: TD metric calculation and region classification. The RGB image is converted into XYZ color space and the TD metric is calculated to find dissimilarity between two texture distributions.

In [31], they addressed two different systems for the detection of melanomas in dermoscopy images. The first system used global methods to classify skin lesions, whereas the second system used local features and the bag-of-features classifier.

## 3. Research methodology

This section describes four main stages: preprocessing, segmentation, features extraction, and classification. We have started by reading an RGB image, as for example, as shown in **Figure 1**.

### 3.1 Preprocessing stage

The preprocessing stage consists of four sequential steps described as follows:

#### *3.1.1 Step 1*

For each channel in the RGB image, a 2-D median filtering for noise reduction with mask of size $5 \times 5$ is implemented and their associated results are depicted in **Figure 2**.

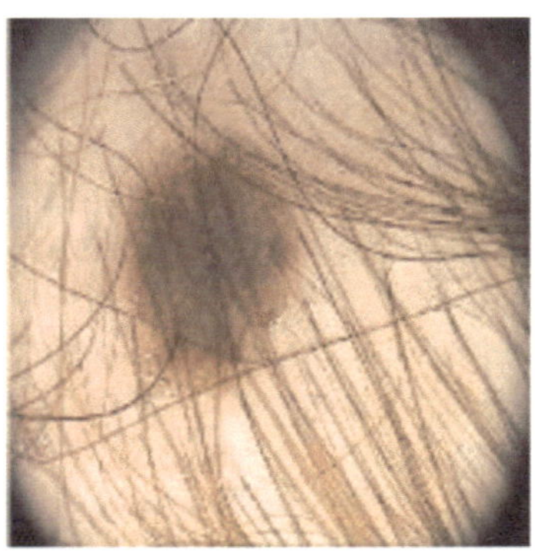

**Figure 1.**
*Input image [32].*

#### 3.1.2 Step 2

For hair removal, two morphological operations are applied on grayscale image f, dilation followed by an erosion with a small shape or template called a structuring element s denoted by ($f \oplus s$ and $f \ominus s$, respectively). The results are depicted in **Figure 3**.

#### 3.1.3 Step 3

Brightness enhancement operation is applied separately on R, G, and B images. **Figure 4** shows the result of the brightness enhancement operation.

#### 3.1.4 Step 4

Based on our experimental studies, the channel B is chosen because it provides better segmentation results compared to others. Therefore, the third channel (B)-image is converted into a binarized form using Otsu's method, and then converted

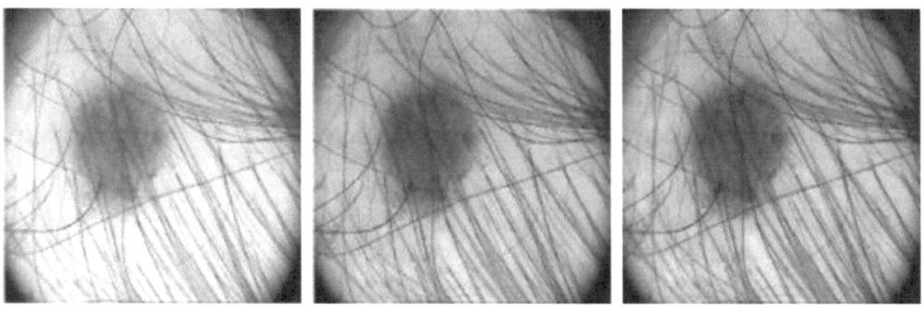

**Figure 2.**
*The implantation of 2-D median filtering. R, G, B-channels, respectively.*

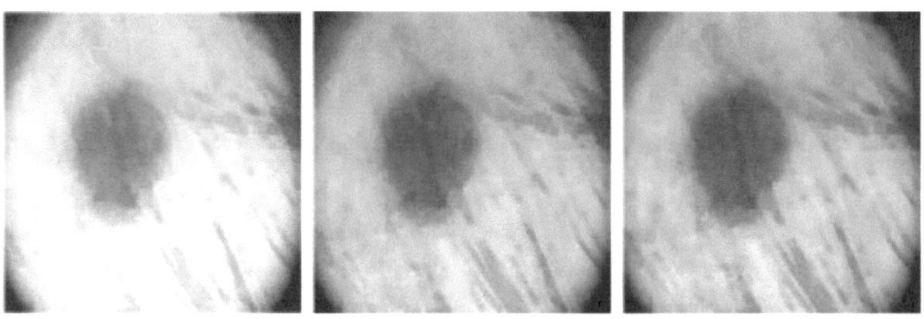

**Figure 3.**
*Hair removal operations. R, G, B-channels, respectively.*

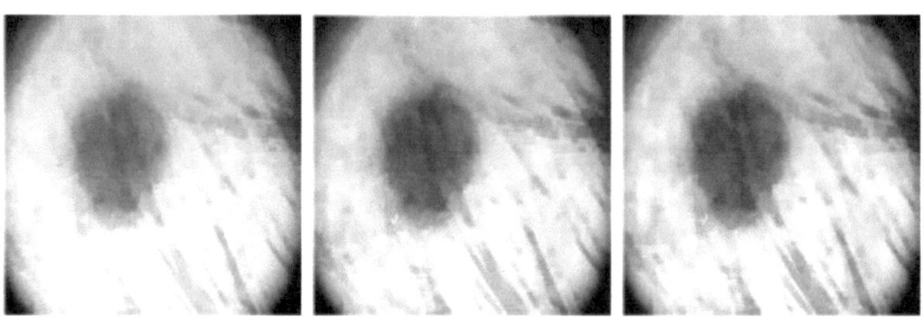

**Figure 4.**
*Brightness enhancement. R, G, B-channels, respectively.*

white pixels into black pixels and vice versa to present the pigment skin lesion. The results of this step are depicted in **Figure 5**.

### 3.2 Segmentation stage

For each candidate region, the statistical properties such as center of mass $(x_c, y_c)$ and area A are calculated. Based on the size of the region and the overlapping with the center of mass of the image, the region-of-interest (ROI) is identified as depicted in **Figure 6**.

### 3.3 Features extraction stage

This section presents and discusses in detail the methods used to extract the four features asymmetry (A), border irregularity (B), color (C), and diameter (D) from the segmented lesion. According to characteristics of the ABCD rule, each extracted feature plays a distinctive role with its associative weight to calculate the total dermoscopy score (TDS).

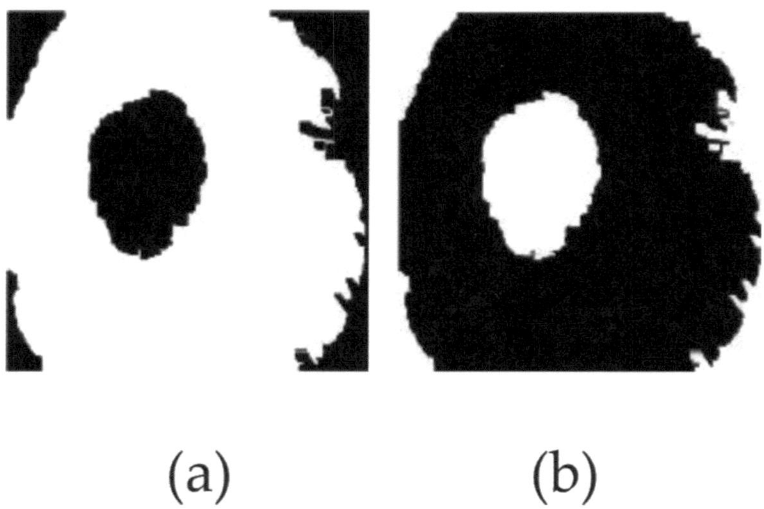


**Figure 5.**
*Binarized images: (a) implementation of Ostu's method and (b) the complement image.*

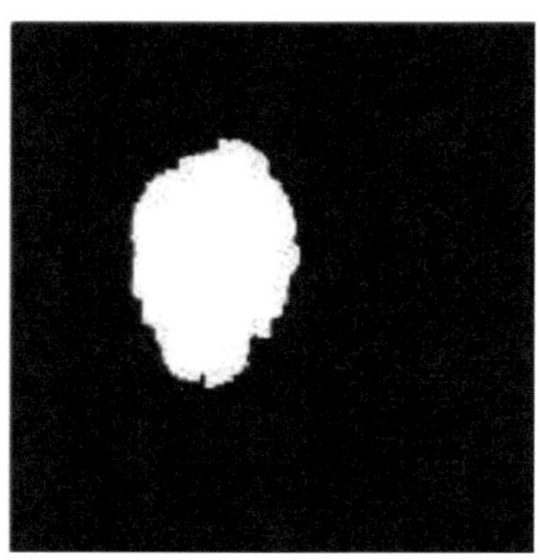

**Figure 6.**
*ROI segmentation.*

### *3.3.1 Asymmetry*

To calculate asymmetry, firstly, the skin lesion is converted into grayscale values. Secondly, it is rotated to vertically and horizontally partitioned into two equal halves. Finally, two methods called Entropy and Bi-fold are implemented, and their calculated average value is assigned as an asymmetry score of the segmented lesion.

Compared with **Figure 6**, the ROI is rotated by $\theta^{\circ}$ to align the $(x, y)$ coordinated with centroid principal axes as shown in **Figure 7**. The orientation angle $\theta^{\circ}$ is defined as the angle between the $x$-axis and axis around which the object can be rotated with minimum inertia:

$$\theta = \frac{1}{2}\arctan\left(\frac{2m_{1,1}}{m_{2,0}-m_{0,2}}\right) \tag{1}$$

where $m_{1,1}$, $m_{2,0}$, and $m_{0,2}$ are the second order moments or moment of inertia defined as:

$$m_{p,q} = \sum_i (x_i - x_0)^p\,(y_i - y_0)^q \tag{2}$$

where $(x_0, y_0)$ is the centroid.

**Figure 8** shows the result of the partition operation of the ROI over its closest line of symmetry (i.e., centroid) into two equal parts vertically and horizontally.

**Figure 7.**
*Alignment operation.*

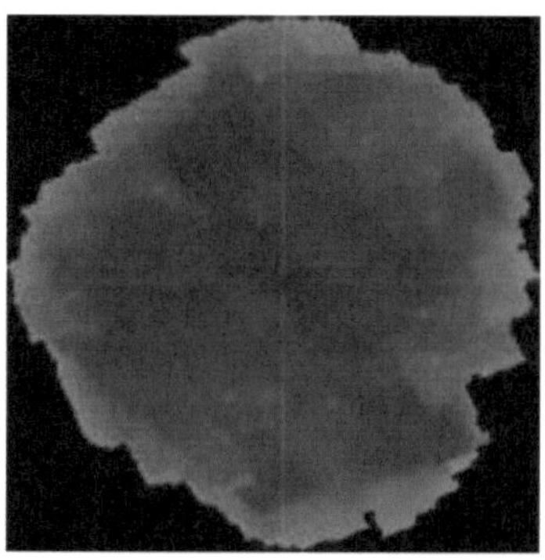

**Figure 8.**
*Vertical and horizontal bisections.*

The asymmetry feature plays an important role in melanoma diagnosis and for this reason we have suggested two methods for implementation:

*3.3.1.1 Entropy function*

The entropy is a statistical measure of randomness that can be used to characterize the texture of grayscale image as described by the following:

$$-\sum p.\,log_2(p) \tag{3}$$

where $p$ contains the histogram counts of intensity values.

To find the similarity between the two parts (left vs. right and upper vs. lower) of the segmented lesion, their entropies are calculated as follows:

$$E_{(L,R)} = \frac{1}{1+|E_L - E_R|} \tag{4}$$

The same process is repeated to find the $E_{(U,\ L)}$. Therefore, the entropy asymmetry is calculated as follows:

$$E_A = \begin{cases} 0, & E_{(L,R)} \geq T_E \ AND \ E_{(U,L)} \geq T_E \\ 1, & E_{(L,R)} \geq T_E \ OR \ E_{(U,L)} \geq T_E \\ 2, & Otherwise \end{cases} \tag{5}$$

where $T_E$ is the entropy threshold value.

*3.3.1.2 Bi-fold method*

The symmetry obtained by overlapping the two vertical (left vs. right) and horizontal (upper vs. lower) parts along the principal axes of the inertia. The non-overlapped is then compared with the total area of the lesion as follows:

$$OVL = \frac{\Delta A}{A} \tag{6}$$

where ΔA is the non-overlapping area between the original and reflected masks and A is the area of the original mask. The result of the non-overlapping operation between left and right halves is depicted in **Figure 9a** and the result of the non-overlapping operation between upper and right halves is depicted in **Figure 9b** as well. Hence, the overlapping asymmetry is calculated as follows:

$$O_A = \begin{cases} 0, & OVL_{(L,R)} \leq T_O \ AND \ OVL_{(U,L)} \leq T_O \\ 1, & OVL_{(L,R)} \leq T_O \ OR \ OVL_{(U,L)} \leq T_O \\ 2, & Otherwise \end{cases} \tag{7}$$

where $T_O$ is an overlapping threshold value.

The overall asymmetry score ($Asym_{Score}$) of the skin lesion is calculated as:

$$Asym_{Score} = \frac{E_A + O_A}{2} \tag{8}$$

### *3.3.2 Border irregularity*

From the binarized ROI (see **Figure 7**), the border irregularity index or compactness index is calculated as follows:

$$Compact\ Index(CI) = \frac{P^2}{2\pi A} \tag{9}$$

where $P$ is the perimeter and $A$ is the area of the lesion.

Among other edge detection methods, Sobel method is selected because it is relatively inexpensive in terms of computations. On the other hand, the gradient approximation that it produces is relatively crude, in particular for high-frequency variations in the image. As shown in **Figure 10**, the lesion's boundary image is partitioned into eight equal segments and for each segment, we have computed its compact index.

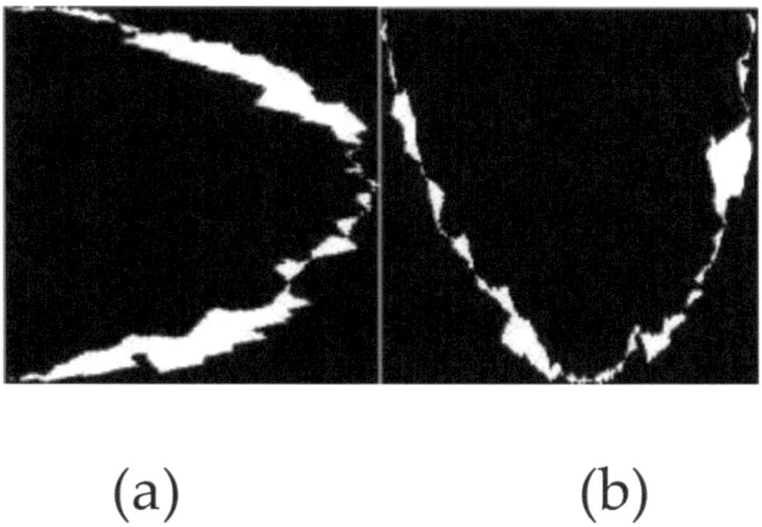

**Figure 9.**
*Non-overlapping area: (a) left-right folding and (b) upper-lower folding.*

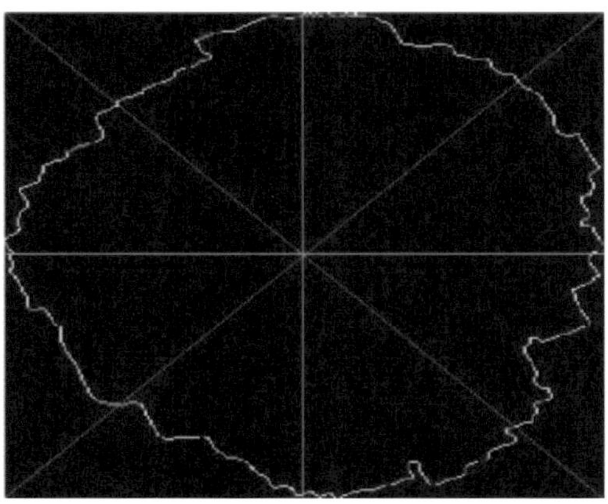

**Figure 10.**
*The result of the partitioning process.*

The border irregularity index ($BI_{Score}$) is calculated as follows:

$$BI_{Score} = \sum_{i=1}^{8} CI_i \tag{10}$$

### 3.3.3 Color feature

The existence of white, black, red, light-brown, dark-brown, and blue-gray colors in the true colored lesion are needed to be examined. Assume that **Figure 11** presents the lesion that is needed to be examined for the six candidate colors appearance. The color score is incremented by 1, if the distance between the examined pixel's value in the lesion and each color reference is below or equal to the pre-calculated threshold value.

Six RGB codes are chosen as reference points for each color used as shown in **Table 1**.

The distance of each pixel in the lesion and color reference is calculated by using the following Euclidean distance:

$$D_k = \sqrt{(r_k - r_{ij})^2 + (g_k - g_{ij})^2 + (b_k - b_{ij})^2} \tag{11}$$

where $k = 1, 2, \ldots, 6$ and $(i, j)$ is the pixel's position in the lesion.

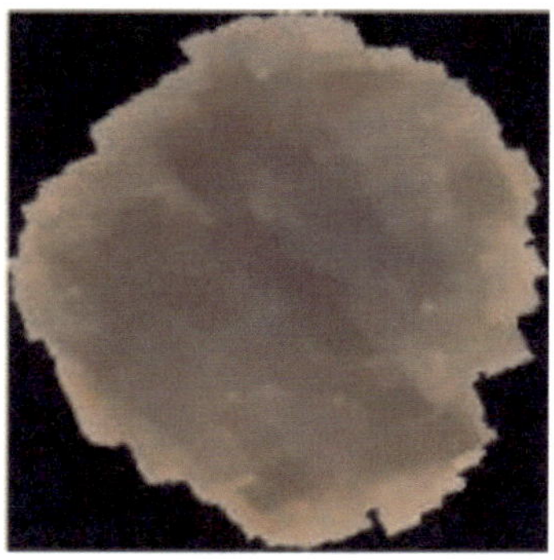

**Figure 11.**
*The examined lesion.*

| White | Black | Red | Light-brown | Dark-brown | Blue-gray |
|---|---|---|---|---|---|
| (1, 1, 1) | (0, 0, 0) | (1, 0, 0) | (0.7843, 0.5882, 0.3922) | (0.5882, 0.3922, 0.3922) | (0.5882, 0.4902, 0.5882) |
| (0.9608, 0.9608, 0.9608) | (0.0392, 0.0392, 0.0392) | (1, 0.1961, 0.1961) | (0.7843, 0.3922, 0) | (0.4902, 0.2941, 0.2941) | (0.4902, 0.4902, 0.5882) |
| (0.9216, 0.9216, 0.9216) | (0.0784, 0.0784, 0.0784) | (0.7843, 0, 0) | (0.7843, 0.3922, 0.1961) | (0.3922, 0.1961, 0.1961) | (0.3922, 0.3922, 0.4902) |
| (0.8824, 0.8824, 0.8824) | (0.1176, 0.1176, 0.1176) | (0.7843, 0.1961, 0.1961) | (0.5882, 0.3922, 0.1961) | (0.3922, 0.1961, 0) | (0.3922, 0.4902, 0.5882) |
| (0.8431, 0.8431, 0.8431) | (0.1569, 0.1569, 0.1569) | (0.5882, 0 0) | (0.5882, 0.3922, 0) | (0.3922, 0, 0) | (0.1961, 0.3922, 0.5882) |
| (0.8039, 0.8039, 0.8039) | (0.1961, 0.1961, 0.1961) | (0.5882, 0.1961, 0.1961) | (0.5882, 0.1961, 0) | (0.1961, 0, 0) | (0, 0.3922, 0.5882) |

**Table 1.**
*RGB codes.*

The existence of colors in lesion depends on the comparison between $D_k$ and threshold values. For each color, there is a threshold value $T_k$ is calculated as a distance between the highest and smallest reference points. As for example, the threshold value for white color (i.e., $T_1$) is calculated as follows:

$$T_1 = \sqrt{3 * (1 - 0.8039)^2} = 0.3397 \tag{12}$$

The same process is repeated for other colors to calculate their threshold values. The color score ($Color_{Score}$) is incremented by 1 if the $D_k \leq T_k$.

### 3.3.4 Diameter

The number of pixels of the greatest diameter or major axis length of the segmented lesion is transferred into millimeter scale as follows:

$$M = \frac{major\ axis\ length * 25.4}{20 * dpi} \tag{13}$$

where *dpi* is the dots-per-inch which equals to 96. Then, the diameter score ($DM_{Score}$) is calculated as follows:

$$DM_{Score} = \begin{cases} 0.5, & M < 2mm \\ 1, & M < 3mm \\ \vdots & \vdots \\ 4.5, & M < 10mm \\ 5, & Otherwise \end{cases} \tag{14}$$

Finally, the calculated values of the four extracted features are multiplied by their weights to receive the total dermoscopic score (TDS). The TDS is calculated by the following equation:

$$TDS = Asym_{Score} * 1.3 + BI_{Score} * 0.1 + Color_{Score} * 0.5 + DM_S * 0.5 \tag{15}$$

## 3.4 Classification stage

Based on the result of the TDS, the lesion is classified based of the following criteria:

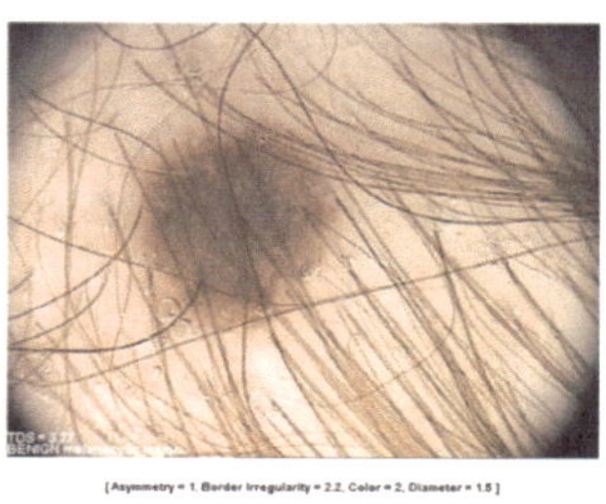


**Figure 12.**
*An example of the implementation of the proposed methodology.*

$$Diagnosis = \begin{cases} Benign, & TDS < 4.75 \\ Suspecious, & TDS \leq 5.45 \\ High\ Suspecious, & Otherwise \end{cases} \tag{16}$$

An example of the whole process yields to the printed results on bottom-left corner of the image is illustrated in **Figure 12**.

## 4. Experimental results and discussion

### 4.1 Hardware and software specifications

The experiments are executed on processor Intel, core i3-2330 M @ 2.20 GHz and RAM 4 GB. The system type is windows 7 ultimate of 64-bit operating and the software used for research implementation is MATLAB R2013a.

### 4.2 Dataset

The performance of our research is tested on $PH^2$ dataset [32]. It consists of 200 8-bit RGB dermoscopic images of melanocytic lesions with a resolution of 768 $\times$ 560 pixels. This image database contains 80 common nevi, 80 atypical nevi, and 40 melanomas. The dermoscopic images were obtained at the Dermatology Service of Hospital Pedro Hispano (Matosinhos, Portugal) under the same conditions through tuebinger mole analyzer system using a magnification of 20 times.

### 4.3 Implementation of ABCD rule

The ABCD rule is implemented on the $PH^2$ dataset and a random selection of segmentation and classification of successful results are presented in **Figure 13**. For each image, the segmented lesion is surrounded by a solid blue line, and the calculated value of the TDS and the classification result are presented in the bottom-left corner.

### 4.4 Discussion

The results of this research are compared with the results of [31], in terms of accuracy, sensitivity, and specificity. The running time for the diagnosis process of 200 8-bit RGB images is 1670 s, or an average of 8.35 s per each examined lesion.

The performance of the proposed work is evaluated by one of the well-known metrics called the confusion matrix as described in **Table 2**. It presents the correct and wrong classification rates that resulted from the implementation of the ABCD rule on $PH^2$ dataset. This image database contains 80 common nevi, 80 atypical nevi, and 40 melanomas.

**Table 3** summarizes the calculated values of true positive (TP), false negative (FN), false positive (FP), and true negative (TN) of the three classes, benign (B), suspicious (S), and high suspicious (H).

The accuracy, sensitivity, and specificity formulas are described in the following equations, respectively. **Table 4** summarizes the achieved performance of the three classes.

*DOI: http://dx.doi.org/10.5772/intechopen.88065*

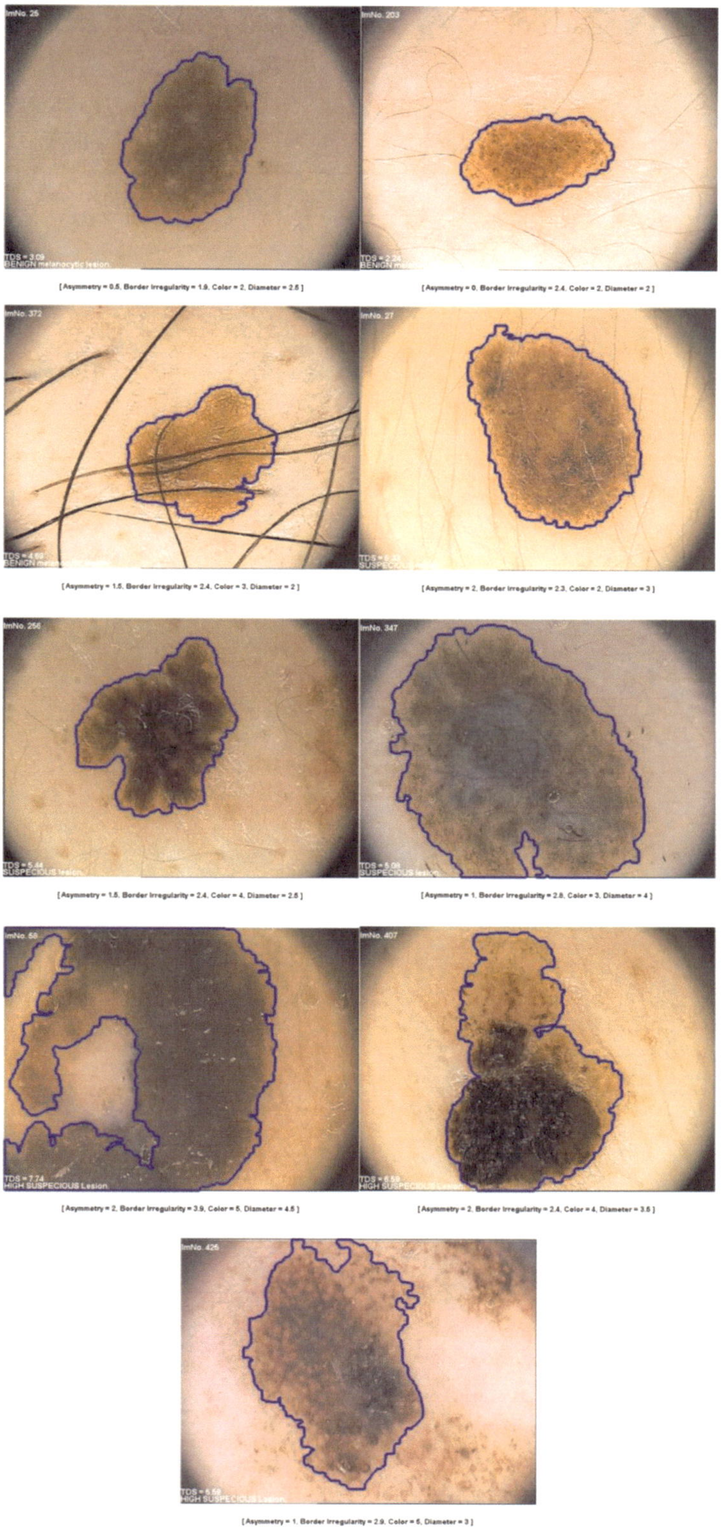


**Figure 13.**
*Results sample.*

| | | Predicted class | | |
|---|---|---|---|---|
| | | **Benign (B)** | **Suspicious (S)** | **High suspicious (H)** |
| Actual class | Benign (B) | TP(B) = 73 | E(BS) = 5 | E(BH) = 2 |
| | Suspicious (S) | E(SB) = 11 | TP(S) = 63 | E(SH) = 6 |
| | High suspicious (H) | E(HB) = 2 | E(HS) = 4 | TP(HS) = 34 |

**Table 2.**
*The ABCD rule performance confusion matrix.*

| | **Benign (B)** | **Suspicious (S)** | **High suspicious (H)** |
|---|---|---|---|
| TP | 73 | 63 | 34 |
| FN | 7 | 17 | 6 |
| FP | 13 | 9 | 8 |
| TN | 107 | 111 | 152 |

**Table 3.**
*Summary of correct and wrong classifications.*

| | **Class** | | | **Average (our work)** | **Average [28]** |
|---|---|---|---|---|---|
| | **B** | **S** | **H** | | |
| Accuracy | 90.00 | 87.00 | 93.00 | 90.00 | — |
| Sensitivity | 91.25 | 78.75 | 85.00 | 85.00 | 98.00 |
| Specificity | 89.17 | 92.50 | 95.00 | 92.22 | 77.50 |

**Table 4.**
*Benchmarking results of the proposed work applied to the $PH^2$ database.*

$$Accuracy = \frac{TP+TN}{TP+FP+FN+TN} \tag{17}$$

$$Sensitivity = \frac{TP}{TP+FN} \tag{18}$$

$$Specificity = \frac{TN}{TN+FP} \tag{19}$$

## 5. Conclusion and future work

In this work, we have developed an automatic diagnostic system using image processing techniques for preliminary diagnosis of melanoma based on the well-proven commonly used ABCD medical procedure. The proposed work used different image processing capabilities to achieve fast, affordable, easily available and highly accurate melanoma diagnosis. The overall process includes multiple modules for handling various steps: noise removal, contrast enhancement, lesion segmentation, features extraction, and classification (diagnosis).

The achieved results show an acceptable performance rates, an accuracy 90%, sensitivity 85%, and specificity 92.22%.

The following opportunities are suggested for future work:

- Increase the size of the dataset, and

- Attach the proposed system to various mobile devices.

## Acknowledgements

The author would like to thank Dr. Saeb Zaqout for his valuable comments and constructive criticism of this manuscript.

## Author details

Ihab Zaqout
Department of Information Technology, Faculty of Engineering and Information Technology, Al-Azhar University, Gaza, Gaza Strip, Palestine

*Address all correspondence to: i.zaqout@alazhar.edu.ps

## References


[1] Melanoma Treatment for Health Professionals (PDQ). National Cancer Institute [Internet]. 2015. Available from: http://www.cancer.gov/types/skin/hp/melanoma-treatment-pdq [Accessed: 29 May 2016]

[2] Stewart BW, Wild CP. World cancer report 2014. World Health Organization, International Agency for Research on Cancer; IARC Publications; 2014

[3] Stolz W, Riemann A, Cognetta A, Braun-Falco O. ABCD rule of dermatoscopy: A new practical method for early recognition of malignant melanoma. European Journal of Dermatology. 1994;**4**(7):521-527

[4] Ahnlide I, Bjellerup M, Nilsson F, Nielsen K. Validity of ABCD rule of dermoscopy in clinical practice. Journal of Acta Dermato-Venereologica. 2016; **96**:367-372. DOI: 10.2340/00015555-2239

[5] Laura RP, Deysi NC, Diego PP-R, José LN, Lizza AT. Computerized medical diagnosis of melanocytic lesions based on the ABCD approach. CLEI Electronic Journal. 2016;**19**(2):1-22. DOI: 10.19153/cleiej.19.2.5

[6] Parker LR. Algorithms for Image Processing and Computer Vision. 2nd ed. Indianapolis, Indiana, USA: Wiley Publishing; 2011

[7] Goodson AG, Grossman D. Strategies for early melanoma detection: Approaches to the patient with nevi. Journal of the American Academy of Dermatology. 2009;**60**(5):719-735. DOI: 10.1016/j.jaad.2008.10.065

[8] Bhuiyan MA, Azad I, Kal-Uddin M. Image processing for skin cancer features extraction. International Journal of Scientific and Engineering Research. 2013; **4**(2):1-6

[9] Jain JW, Ramteke NS. ABCD rule based automatic computer-aided skin cancer detection using MATLAB. International Journal on Computer Technology and Applications. 2013; **4**(4):691-697

[10] Malini M, Saranya DAA. Review of segmentation techniques on melanoma detection. International Journal of Advanced Research in Computer Science and Software Engineering. 2015; **5**(4):1043-1047

[11] Maglogianni I, Kosmopoulos DI. Computational vision systems for the detection of malignant melanoma. Oncology Reports. 2006;**15**:1027-1032

[12] Deserno TM, Ali A. A systematic review of automated melanoma detection in dermatoscopic images and its ground truth data. In: Proceedings of SPIE Medical Imaging, International Society for Optics and Photonics; 2012. p. 8318

[13] D'Amico M, Stanganelli I. Qualitative asymmetry measure for melanoma detection. In: IEEE International Symposium on Biomedical Imaging; 15-18 April 2004; Arlington, VA, USA; 2004. 2: pp. 1155-1158

[14] Cudek P, Grzymała-Busse W, Hippe ZS. Further research on automatic estimation of asymmetry of melanocytic skin lesions. In: Human Computer Systems Interaction: Backgrounds and Applications 2, Advances in Intelligent and Soft Computing Series. Vol. 99. Berlin, Heidelberg: Springer; 2004. pp. 125-129. DOI: 10.1007/978-3-642-23172-8

[15] Ravichandran KS, Premaladha J. Asymmetry analysis of malignant melanoma using image processing: A survey. Journal of Artificial Intelligence. 2014;7(2):45-53. DOI: 10.3923/jai.2014.45.53

[16] Pise N, Jagtap V, Jain S. Computer aided melanoma skin cancer detection using image processing. In: International Conference on Intelligent Computing, Communication & Convergence (ICCC-2015), Elsevier, Procedia Computer Science; December 2015; Bhubaneswar, Odisha, India; 2015. 48: pp. 735-740

[17] Ananthi B, Balamohan S, Hemalatha M. Melanoma detection using RGB color model in medical imaging. Middle-East Journal of Scientific Research. 2014; **21**(11):1982-1987. DOI: 10.5829/idosi.mejsr.2014.21.11.21494

[18] Iqbal S, Sophia J, Divyashree A, Mundas M, Vidya R. Implementation of supervised learning for melanoma detection using image processing. International Journal of Research in Engineering and Technology. 2015;**4**(6): 325-329. DOI: 10.15623/ijret.2015.0406055

[19] Grammatikopoulos G, Hatzigaidas A, Papastergiou A, Lazaridis P, Zaharis Z, Kampitaki D, et al. Automated malignant melanoma detection using MATLAB. In: Proceedings of the 5th WSEAS International Conference on Data Networks, Communications & Computers; 16-17 October 2006; Bucharest, Romania; 2006. pp. 91-94

[20] Iqbal S, Sophia M, Divyashree JA, Mundas M, Vidya R. Implementation of Stolz's algorithm for melanoma detection. International Advanced Research Journal in Science, Engineering and Technology. 2015;**2**(6): 9-12. DOI: 10.14445/23488549/IJECE-V4I4P105

[21] Turkar V, Shetty P. Melanoma decision support system for dermatologist. In: International Conference on Recent Trends in Information Technology and Computer Science (IRCTITCS); 2011. pp. 28-30

[22] Jaiswar S, Kadri M, Gatty V. Skin cancer detection using digital image processing. International Journal of Scientific Engineering and Research (IJSER). 2015;**3**(6):138-140

[23] Situ N, Yuan X, Chen J, Zouridakis G. Malignant melanoma detection by Bag-of-features classification. In: 30th Annual International Conference of the IEEE Engineering in Medicine and Biology Society; 20-25 August 2008; Vancouver, Canada; 2008. pp. 3110-3113

[24] Catarina B, Jorge SM, Teresa M. Bag-of-features classification model for the diagnose of melanoma in dermoscopy images using color and texture descriptors. In: 10th International Conference on Image Analysis and Recognition; 26-28 June 2013; Póvoa do Varzim, Portugal; 2013. pp. 547-555

[25] Cheerla N, Frazier D. Automatic melanoma detection using multi-stage neural networks. International Journal of Innovative Research in Science, Engineering and Technology. 2014;**3**(2): 9164-9183

[26] Aswin RB, Abdul Jaleel J, Salim S. Implementation of ANN classifier using MATLAB for skin cancer detection. In: International Conference on Mobility in Computing-ICMiC13; 17-18 December 2013; India; 2013. pp. 87-94

[27] Messadi M, Cherifi H, Bessaid A-H. Segmentation and ABCD rule extraction for skin tumors classification. Journal of Convergence Information Technology (JCIT). 2014;**9**(2):21-34

[28] Tomatis S, Carraral M, Bono A, Bartoli C, Lualdi M, Tragni G, et al. Automated melanoma detection with a novel multispectral imaging system: Results of a prospective study. Institute of Physics Publishing, Physics in Medicine and Biology. 2005;**50**(8): 1675-1687. DOI: 10.1088/0031-9155/50/8/004

[29] Santiago-Montero R, Hernandez D. Border and asymmetry measuring of skin lesion for diagnostic of melanoma using a perimeter ratio. Asian Journal of Computer Science and Information Technology. 2016;**6**(2):7-13. DOI: 10.15520/ajcsit.v6i2.41

[30] Akila IS, Sumathi V. Detection of melanoma skin cancer using segmentation and classification algorithms. In: Proceedings on National Conference on Information and Communication Technologies (IJCA 2015); 2015. 2: pp. 1-4

[31] Barata C, Ruela M, Francisco M, Mendonça T, Marques J. Two systems for the detection of melanomas in dermoscopy images using texture and color features. IEEE Systems Journal 2013;**99**:1–15. DOI: 10.1109/JSYST. 2013.2271540.

[32] $PH^2$ dataset [Internet]. 2016. Available from: https://www.dropbox.com/s/k88qukc20ljnbuo/PH2Dataset.rar [Accessed: 12 May 2016]

Chapter 7

# Novel Formulation of Parzen Data Analysis

*David Horn*


## Abstract

The Parzen analysis associates Gaussian kernels with each data point, thus obtaining a density function which may be viewed as a possible artificial generator of the data. This probability function can be decomposed into the product of two components, weight (W) and shape (S), which represent different aspects of the data. We demonstrate how this naturally leads to a formalism of fields in data space, which are interconnected through relations in one-dimensional scale space, corresponding to the common Gaussian width. We discuss the connection of this formalism to different clustering procedures such as quantum clustering (QC) and mean shift (MS). We demonstrate on various examples the importance of these concepts in the analysis of natural data as well as in image analysis in two or three dimensions.


**Keywords:** Parzen probability, weight-shape decomposition, quantum clustering, mean shift, image analysis

## 1. Introduction

Unsupervised machine learning has led to a wealth of clustering methods over the past few decades [1]. One of the important early ideas is that of the Parzen window distribution [2]. It has been introduced in 1962, as a kernel density estimate of a distribution function underlying measured data, and still serves as the basis of clustering algorithms in pattern recognition [1, 3]. Recently, it has been discovered [4] that the Parzen probability function can be decomposed into two components, weight and shape, which represent different aspects of the data. Weight, as its name implies, describes the semi-global strength of the distribution, whereas shape represents local properties which come to light once the bias of the weight is being removed. Moreover, $-\log(\text{shape})$ coincides with a potential function V, which has been previously introduced in quantum clustering (QC) [5]. The cluster centers in QC correspond to minima of V. An alternative method, mean shift [6, 7], views the maxima of the probability function as the appropriate candidates of cluster centers. These two different points of view can now be studied and compared within a unified formalism [4].

Here we discuss the novel connections of the Parzen distribution to its potential and show how both can be used for the analysis of data points, leading to alternative clustering possibilities and extracting interesting features from the data. A particularly interesting set of applications appears in image analysis. Scale-space image analysis [8] has developed from the Parzen kernel methodology discussed in [6].



IntechOpen

Now it turns out that insights from the potential term, or the shape component, allow for novel applications which are relevant to medical and technical imaging.

## 2. The Parzen probability distribution and its potential function

Data analysis often involves dimensionality reduction and noise removal, as well as some other tools, which eventually lead to consider a set of preprocessed data points located in a d-dimensional Euclidean space $\mathbf{x}_i \in \mathbb{R}^d$, with possible positive attributes (e.g., intensities) $I_i$. For this set, we define the non-normalized Parzen window function with Gaussian kernels as

$$\psi_\sigma(\mathbf{x}) = \sum_i I_i e^{-\frac{(\mathbf{x}-\mathbf{x}_i)^2}{2\sigma^2}} \tag{1}$$

Following [4], we introduce a relative probability weight function representing the influence of the kernel at data point $\mathbf{x}_i$ on any arbitrary point $\mathbf{x}$:

$$p_i(\mathbf{x}) = \frac{e^{-\frac{(\mathbf{x}-\mathbf{x}_i)^2}{2\sigma^2}}}{\psi(\mathbf{x})} \tag{2}$$

It obeys $\sum_i I_i p_i(\mathbf{x}) = 1$ and allows for the definition of two new scalar functions over data space $\mathbf{x}$, which are the potential and entropy fields

$$V(\mathbf{x}) = \sum_i I_i \frac{(\mathbf{x}-\mathbf{x}_i)^2}{2\sigma^2} p_i(\mathbf{x}) \tag{3}$$

$$H(\mathbf{x}) = -\sum_i I_i p_i(\boldsymbol{x}) \log p_i(\mathbf{x}) \tag{4}$$

Their difference is related to the Parzen probability function

$$V(\mathbf{x}) = \mathrm{H}(\mathbf{x}) - \log \psi(\mathbf{x}) \tag{5}$$

This can be rewritten as

$$\psi(\mathbf{x}) = W(\mathbf{x}) S(\mathbf{x}) \tag{6}$$

using [4] the concepts of weight and shape: $W(\mathbf{x}) = e^{H(\mathbf{x})}$ and $S(\mathbf{x}) = e^{-V(\mathbf{x})}$.

Since $V(\mathbf{x}) \geq 0$, it follows that $S(\mathbf{x}) \leq 1$. Moreover, both $W$ and $S$ are nonnegative. $S$ is integrable over $\mathbf{x}$ and, as such, can also serve as a distribution. From the definitions of (1) and (3), one can derive [4] the Schrödinger equation

$$-\frac{\sigma^2}{2}\nabla^2\psi(\mathbf{x}) + V(\mathbf{x})\psi(\mathbf{x}) = \frac{d}{2}\psi(\mathbf{x}), \tag{7}$$

which has been the cornerstone of the QC algorithm [5].

## 3. Interplay of scale and data space dependence

All the scalar fields over data space, introduced in the previous section, depend on the parameter σ, the scale of all Gaussian kernels. This dependence leads to further interesting relations between the Parzen probability function and its potential. Thus, from the definitions (1) and (3), it follows that

$$\frac{\sigma}{2}\frac{\partial}{\partial\sigma}\log\psi_\sigma(\mathbf{x}) = V_\sigma(\mathbf{x}) \tag{8}$$

where we keep the index σ which has been suppressed in the previous section. This relation displays a direct connection between the two scalar functions defining the probability and the potential. We proceed now to introduce a vector field $\mathbf{D}_\sigma$ which is defined by

$$-\nabla\log\psi_\sigma(\mathbf{x}) = \mathbf{D}_\sigma \tag{9}$$

and vanishes when the probability reaches its extrema in data space. Interestingly it is also related to the gradient of the potential function, through

$$\frac{-\sigma}{2}\frac{\partial}{\partial\sigma}\mathbf{D}_\sigma = \nabla V_\sigma \tag{10}$$

Hence we conclude that the potential reaches its extrema when $\mathbf{D}_\sigma$ remains stationary with respect to variations of σ.

$\mathbf{D}_\sigma$ may be expressed, in analogy with Eq. (3), as

$$\mathbf{D}(\mathbf{x}) = \sum_i I_i \frac{\mathbf{x}-\mathbf{x}_i}{\sigma^2} p_i(\mathbf{x}). \tag{11}$$

Its square $U = \mathbf{D}^2$ serves as an indicator function whose stationarity

$$\frac{\sigma}{2}\frac{\partial}{\partial\sigma}U_\sigma(\mathbf{x}) = 2\nabla\log\psi_\sigma(\mathbf{x})\cdot\nabla V_\sigma(\mathbf{x}) = 0 \tag{12}$$

implies the existence of extrema of either the probability or the potential. Since $U = \mathbf{D}^2$ is nonnegative, $U = 0$ is a minimum in σ. It corresponds to extrema of $\psi$ which are associated with $\mathbf{D}=0$. Other values of $U$ which obey Eq. (12) are associated with extrema of $V$ which occur whenever $\frac{\partial}{\partial\sigma}\mathbf{D}_\sigma = 0$.Eq. (12) may be viewed as a statement concerning a set of points of interest in the data: all extrema of either the probability or the potential. In analogy with statistics, one may also view this equation as an inference method finding the parameter $\sigma$ which leads to points of interest at given values of $\mathbf{x}$.

Although all extrema may be regarded as points of interest, some are of more interest than others: extrema that remain fixed in $\mathbf{x}$ for a range of scale values, which is large compared with the range of scales of other points of interest. This criterion, introduced by Roberts [9], allows searching for scales which correspond to natural properties of the data. Thus it subserves the search for good clustering of the data [4, 5, 9].

Finally, we wish to point out that $\psi$ is not a properly normalized distribution function. A proper probability function, whose integral is 1, is defined by

$$P = \frac{1}{N}\left(\frac{1}{2\pi\sigma^2}\right)^{\frac{d}{2}}\psi(\mathbf{x}) \tag{13}$$

where $N = \sum_i I_i$. We note that $\psi$ and $V$ obey a joint integration constraint [10]

$$\frac{1}{N}\left(\frac{1}{2\pi\sigma^2}\right)^{\frac{d}{2}}\int d\mathbf{x}\psi(\mathbf{x})V(\mathbf{x}) = \frac{d}{2}. \tag{14}$$

This may be interpreted as a constraint on the expectation value of the potential function in data space.

Examples of the behavior of $\log\psi$ and of $V$ are demonstrated in **Figure 1** for a data set of 9000 observed galaxies (with redshift in the domain $0.47 \pm 0.005$) regarded as points in spherical angles θ and φ within some limited range. Whereas for $\sigma = 2$ (in units of angle degrees), the two fields exhibit many extrema; there exist clear differences for larger sigma, for example, σ = 10, where $\log\psi$ has one maximum, while $V$ displays several minima. This figure is taken from [10], a paper which contains a detailed and expanded formulation of the analysis presented in this section.

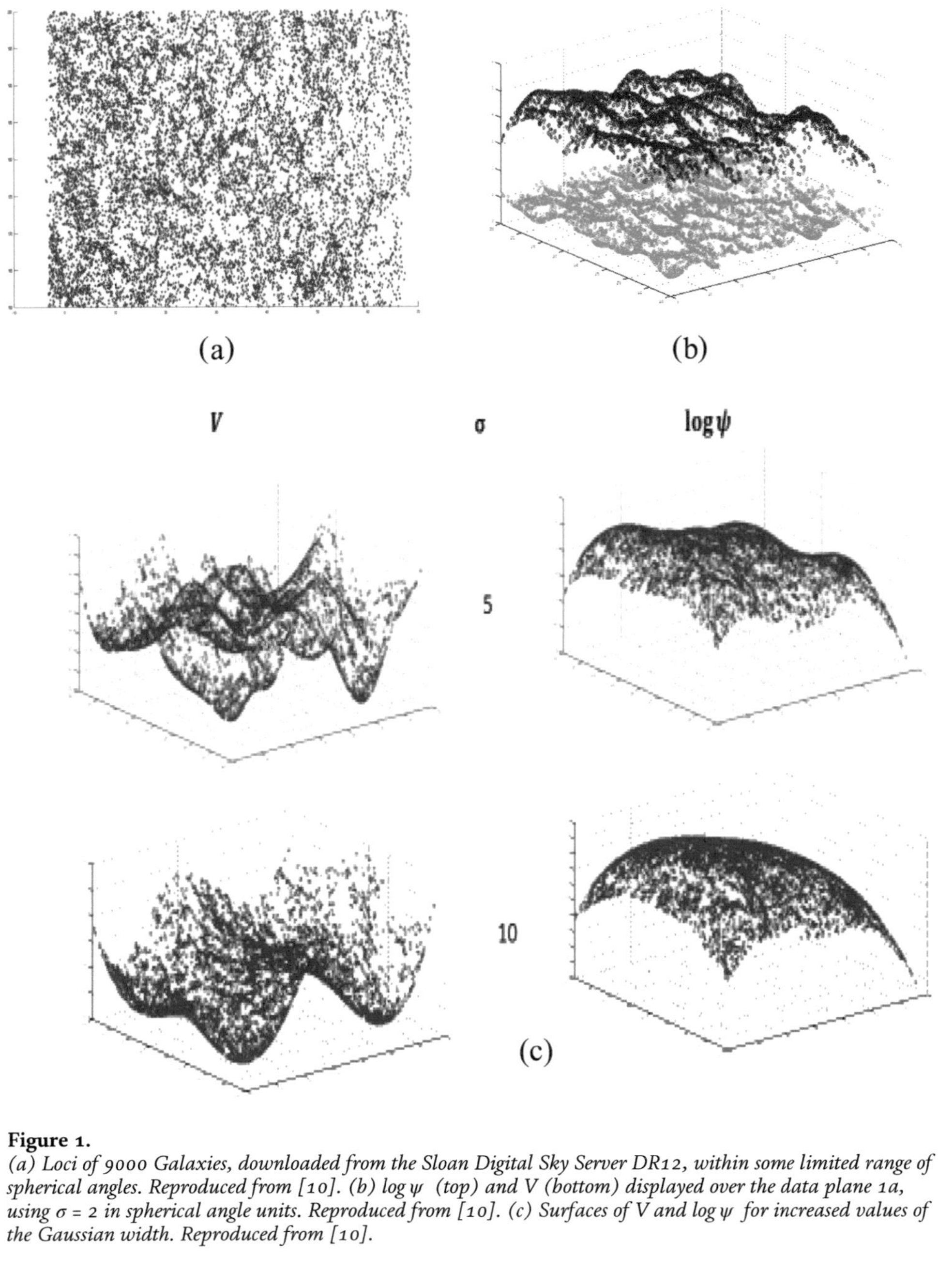


**Figure 1.**
*(a) Loci of 9000 Galaxies, downloaded from the Sloan Digital Sky Server DR12, within some limited range of spherical angles. Reproduced from [10]. (b)* $\log\psi$ *(top) and V (bottom) displayed over the data plane 1a, using* $\sigma = 2$ *in spherical angle units. Reproduced from [10]. (c) Surfaces of V and* $\log\psi$ *for increased values of the Gaussian width. Reproduced from [10].*

## 4. Applications to clustering, image analysis, and more

### 4.1 Anomalies

**Figure 1** serves as an example of different behaviors of $\log \psi$ and of $V$. We wish to stress that when studying this system with large σ, the probability distribution is smooth; nonetheless underlying structure is observed in $V$. This means that, for a given σ, representing the large-scale behavior with one Gaussian, as one may be tempted to do after seeing the probability distribution, is wrong as demonstrated by the structures observed in $V$. On the other hand, the probability function tends to a smooth limit for σ = 10, whereas the fluctuating $V$ changes with σ; hence $V$ may represent random fluctuations in the data. However, comparing with the raw data in **Figure 1a**, we can be convinced that structure of the type discovered by $V$ exists in the data. If these are fluctuations or not, one cannot tell from a single set of data.

A generally important question is if, within changing patterns of $V$, there exists one (or some) which remains relatively stable as function of σ. Such a structure may be viewed as a possible anomaly in the data. It is therefore advisable to study $V$ when looking for anomalies.

### 4.2 Clustering

Clustering methodologies based on maximization of the probability and minimization of the potential can be defined by letting replica of data points move in these directions. These methods are known as mean shift (MS) and quantum clustering (QC) correspondingly. A recent review of MS techniques has been presented in [11]. Analyzing the same data with the same width-parameter σ leads to different clustering results for these two different methods, as is expected from **Figure 1**.

For illustration of clustering based on these different methods, we consider the crab data set which is included in Ripley's textbook [12]. It consists of 200 instances belonging to four equally sized classes and is defined in a five-dimensional parameter space. Performing PCA and restricting ourselves to the 2D plane defined by PC2-PC3 lead to a challenging clustering problem which has been discussed by [13], when introducing support vector clustering (SVC), and by [5] when introducing QC. It has been used in other papers employing variations of QC, such as the recent study [14]. Here we will show the results of [4] who applied to these data three clustering methods: Maximal Shape Clustering (MSC) which coincides with QC, Maximal Probability Clustering (MPC) which coincides with MS, and Maximal Entropy Clustering (MEC). The quality of all three methods may be judged by applying the Jaccard score

$$J = \frac{\mathbf{n}_{11}}{\mathbf{n}_{11} + \mathbf{n}_{10} + \mathbf{n}_{01}}$$

where $n_{11}$ is the number of pairs of points which belong together both in the same class (accepted as "ground truth") and in the same cluster, while $n_{10} + n_{01}$ are numbers of pairs which belong to the same class but different clusters and vice versa. This test is performed in **Figure 2a**, demonstrating that QC wins the competition for a wide range of σ values. The expected asymptotic value is J = 98/398, befitting one cluster and four classes.

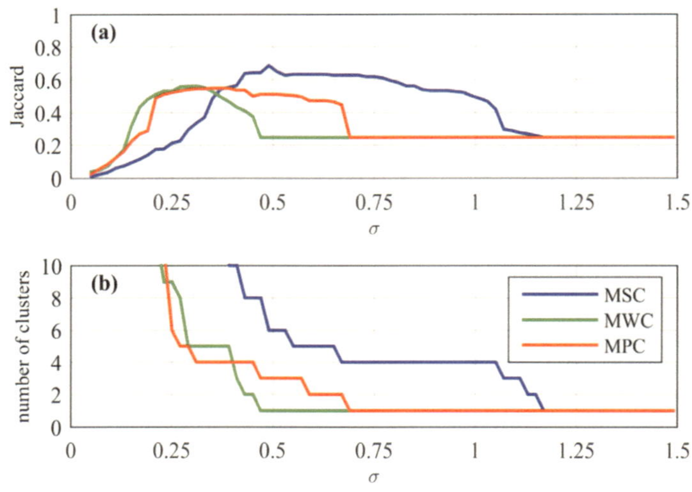


**Figure 2.**
*(a) The Jaccard score, comparing clustering results with expert classification, comparing three clustering methods over a range of σ values. (b) The number of clusters, for each method and value of σ. Reproduced from [4]. MSC, MWC, and MPC stand for maximal shape, weight, and probability clustering accordingly. MSC coincides with quantum clustering and MPC with mean shift.*

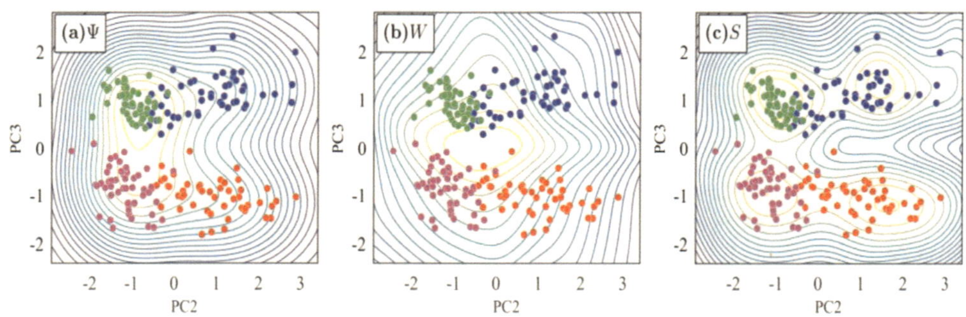


**Figure 3.**
*Topographic maps of probability, weight, and shape, for σ = 0.7. Reproduced from [4].*

Another comparison is being made in **Figure 2b**. This follows Roberts' criterion [9] that the preferable clustering method is the one which displays the most stable number of clusters with respect to variation of σ. This criterion is handy when the ground truth is unknown. QC excels also in this test, leading to a stable prediction of four clusters for a wide range of σ. This last figure also serve as a credibility test for Roberts' criterion.

In order to make the clustering results more intuitive, we display in **Figure 3**, also taken from [4], topographic maps of the different fields describing probability, weight, and shape, for σ = 0.7. The points in four different colors represent the four different classes. The topographic maps allow one to understand the clustering results which represent the outcome of gradient ascent applied to replica of data points which climb toward their nearest peak. Comparing the topologies of **Figure 3** with the results for σ = 0.7 in **Figure 2** leads to an understanding of why the three methods differ from each other.

### 4.3 Image analysis

A gray-scale image may be analyzed as a set of inputs associated with different pixels. In higher dimensional problems, such as 3D MRI data, the pixels are replaced by voxels. Both may fit well into our analysis which starts with Eq. (1), associating a probability distribution with every image. One may then wonder if the weight-shape decomposition of Eq. (6)

$$\psi(\mathbf{x}) = W(\mathbf{x})S(\mathbf{x})$$

can lead to any novel understanding of image analysis.

In any practical application, non-normalized probability and weight may have very large amplitudes, yet shape will be limited to values $\leq 1$. Nonetheless it carries some important characteristics:

1. Shape may be normalized to become a distribution on its own.

2. Shape serves as a generalized edge detector.

3. Shape is the basis of QC; hence the latter is very relevant to clustering of regions where shape is large. Alternative methods may be relevant when shape is small.

The first claim is trivial since $S$ is limited to the range $0 \leq S \leq 1$, and the Gaussian kernels are integrable. The second property is a result of Eq. (7) which shows that the potential is related to the second derivative of the probability. It has led to an interesting result in [4], demonstrating that line caricatures of images can be produced by thresholded shape drawings.

To demonstrate the third point, we display in **Figure 4** the results of an analysis of a T2 MRI of the brain of a Macaque monkey [15]. Following the general procedure outlined above, and limiting ourselves to large relative values (thresholded distributions) of probability and shape, we find that the latter peaks in cortical regions, whereas the former peaks in internal regions of the brain, as demonstrated in **Figure 4**. Thus, a simple thresholding procedure allows one to easily segment the MR image, for the purpose of further analysis of the cortex by applying QC to the data in the large $S$ domain. In **Figure 5**, we follow these conclusions [15] with a display of QC clusters projected onto the surface of the brain, leading to its

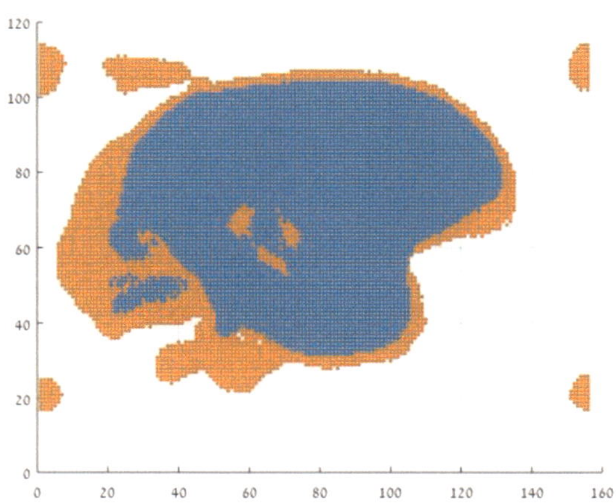


**Figure 4.**
*Thresholded shape (red) and thresholded probability (blue) dominate different regions within the same MR image of a macaque brain, projected on its y-z plane. This analysis used σ = 3 in voxel units. Data outside the brain are due to artifacts and noise in the MR image. These results are due to [15], and they indicate that large shape components dominate cortical regions of the T2 MRI brain image.*

parcellation into cortical components which are derived by just computational image analysis.

### 4.4 Convolutional representation of $V$

When one analyzes data in a regular underlying structure, such as pixels $\mathbf{m}$ of an image $I(\mathbf{m})$, the translational invariance of the Gaussian kernel allows one to use a convolutional description such as

$$\psi[\mathbf{m}] = \sum_{\mathbf{n}} I[\mathbf{n}]K[\mathbf{m}-\mathbf{n}] = I * K[\mathbf{m}] \tag{15}$$

with $K$ being a discrete representation of the kernel. This leads [4] to the following result for the potential

$$V[\mathbf{m}] = \frac{I * L[\mathbf{m}]}{I * K[\mathbf{m}]} \tag{16}$$

where $L = -K \log K$. Such 3D kernels were applied to brain MR images [15] leading to the results displayed in **Figures 4** and 5.

Noting that Eq. (15) is reminiscent of a convolutional layer in a deep network [16], we hypothesize that it can be useful to incorporate intermediate layers with nonlinear filters such as Eq. (16), as additional non-trained pooling filters in deep networks.

### 4.5 Computational remarks

The clustering methodology which has been employed in the different examples shown above is the simplest flavor of gradient descent (or ascent). It calculates the relevant fields on the basis of the data points and continues with straightforward dynamics that have been applied to replica of data points, seeking the extrema of the fields. Various alternatives to this basic application exist. The most important one is hierarchical clustering, which allows for conceptual simplicity and saves computational complexity. Such methodologies were described and discussed in [11] and in [4].

Computational complexity is an obvious issue when working with large data sets. Thus, 3D MRI data may easily comprise 1 M points, whereas their

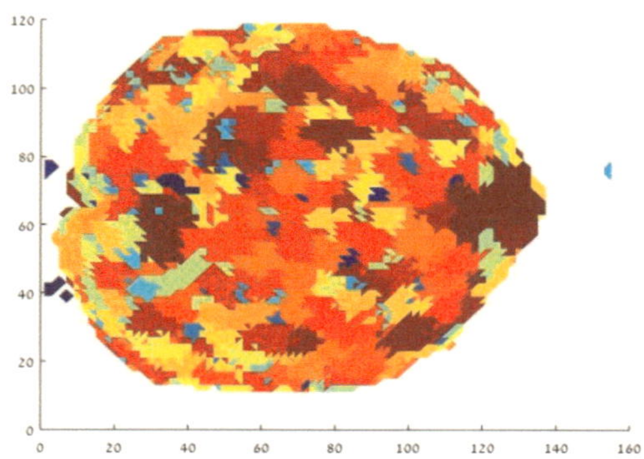


**Figure 5.**
*Characteristic results of QC cortical clusters as mapped onto the surface of the brain and projected onto the x-y plane. This figure displays a map of the largest clusters of shape, each described by a different color. These results are due to Fisher [15].*

manipulation within a system like MATLAB may well be limited to handling only 40 K points at a time [15]. One way to overcome such issues is to consider performing the analysis within extended voxels, for example, voxels containing three pixels in each direction in a 3D image problem. Within each new voxel, one may simply sum the intensity of points, leading to a new presentation of the data in the form of Eq. 1 on the smaller extended voxel space. Clearly one has to make sure that such an approximation does not harm interesting features of the data.

When analyzing other big data, no prior dimensional representation may be required. For the sake of noise reduction and computational complexity, it is advantageous to first apply relevant dimensional reduction, as provided, for example, by singular value decomposition (SVD) and principal component analysis (PCA). It is also important to make sure that the different axes are of similar scale, as shown in the example of **Figure 3**. When the data is still large, one may apply the trick of extended voxels described above. For very large data, one may also separate the data into several components, as is customary in supervised learning, to make sure that conclusions are not affected by the random choice of a subset of the data.

## 5. Conclusions

In the past (see, e.g., [3]), Parzen analysis has not considered the potential field $V$, which plays an important part in the understanding of different features of the data. In particular, $V$ is sensitive to small changes in the Parzen probability by being related to its second derivative. It is also the basis of quantum clustering whose advantages have been demonstrated here as well as in many other investigations in the literature. The discovery of the weight-shape decomposition of the Parzen probability has led to a focus on shape and on the potential and allows for a meaningful comparative discussion of the different features which may be extracted from data.

Here we have defined a set of fields in data space which hopefully will turn out to serve as useful tools in future data analyses. They seem to be adequately applicable to image analysis, and we expect them to be particularly useful in biomedical and technical image analyses in three dimensions. When analyzing other data, where no visual display constraints exist, noise reduction and computational complexity call for preprocessing by dimensional reduction. Further reduction of computational complexity may be tried by employing extended voxels, which our technique can easily accommodate.

In summary, this extended Parzen method replaces any set of discreet data by a continuous set of fields in data space, with interrelations in scale space. It allows for investigating data properties in terms of these fields and their extrema.

## Acknowledgements

This work has been partially supported by the Blavatnik Cyber Center of Tel Aviv University. I thank Itay Fisher for his help with numerical data analysis.

## Conflict of interest

The author declares no conflict of interest.

## Author details

David Horn
Sackler School of Physics and Astronomy, Tel Aviv University, Tel Aviv, Israel

*Address all correspondence to: horn@tau.ac.il

## References

[1] Xu D, Tian Y. A comprehensive survey of clustering algorithms. Annals of Data Science. 2015;**2**(2):165-193

[2] Parzen E. On estimation of a probability density function and mode. The Annals of Mathematical Statistics. 1962;**33**(3):1065-1076

[3] Duda RO, Hart PE, Stork DG. Pattern Classification. 2nd ed. New York: Wiley-Interscience; 2001

[4] Deutsch L, Horn D. The weight-shape decomposition of density estimates: A framework for clustering and image analysis algorithms. Pattern Recognition. 2018;**81**:190-199

[5] Horn D, Gottlieb A. Algorithm for data clustering in pattern recognition problems based on quantum mechanics. Physical Review Letters. 2001;**88**(1): 018702

[6] Cheng Y. Mean shift, mode seeking, and clustering. IEEE Transactions on Pattern Analysis and Machine Intelligence. 1995;**17**(8):790-799

[7] Comaniciu D, Meer P. Mean shift: A robust approach toward feature space analysis. IEEE Transactions on Pattern Analysis and Machine Intelligence. 2002;**24**(5):603-619

[8] Lindeberg T. Scale-space theory: A basic tool for analyzing structures at different scales. Journal of Applied Statistics. 1994;**21**(1–2):225-270

[9] Roberts SJ. Parametric and non-parametric unsupervised cluster analysis. Pattern Recognition. 1997; **30**(2):261-272

[10] Horn D. Field Formulation of Parzen Data Analysis. arXiv eprint 1808.08776. 2018

[11] Carreira-Perpiñán MA. Clustering methods based on kernel density estimators: Mean-shift algorithms. In: Hennig C, Meila M, Murtagh F, Rocci R, editors. Invited chapter in Handbook of Cluster Analysis. Chapter 18. UK: CRC/ Chapman and Hall (Taylor & Francis Group); 2015. pp. 383-418

[12] Ripley BD. Pattern Recognition and Neural Networks. Cambridge, UK: Cambridge University Press; 1996

[13] Ben-Hur A, Horn D, Siegelmann HT, Vapnik V. Support vector clustering. Journal of Machine Learning Research. 2001;**2**(Dec):125-137

[14] Scott TC, Therani M, Wang XM. Data clustering with quantum mechanics. Mathematics. 2017;**5**:5. DOI: 10.3390/math5010005

[15] Fisher I. Parcellation of brain images using shape analysis [M.Sc. thesis]. Tel-Aviv University; 2018. http://horn.tau.ac.il/publications/FisherThesis.pdf

[16] LeCun Y, Bengio Y, Hinton G. Deep learning. Nature. 2015;**521**:436-444